CANON LAW BETWEEN
INTERPRETATION AND IMAGINATION
Monsignor W. Onclin Chair 2001

KATHOLIEKE UNIVERSITEIT LEUVEN
Faculteit Kerkelijk Recht
Faculty of Canon Law

CANON LAW BETWEEN INTERPRETATION AND IMAGINATION

Monsignor W. Onclin Chair 2001

UITGEVERIJ PEETERS
LEUVEN
2001

ISBN 90-429-1005-4
D.2001/0602/28

INHOUDSTAFEL / TABLE OF CONTENTS

NECESSARY CANONICAL REFORM: URGENT ISSUES FOR ACTION

JAMES A. CORIDEN

I have argued here this week that Canon Law is primarily and principally a ministry within the church. It is a ministry circumscribed by the
theology of communion and the concrete realities of congregations of
Christ's faithful. It is a ministry devoted to the maintenance of Christian
freedom and good order within and among particular and local Catholic
churches. Canonical ministry assists in the governance of the church in
the present time, but it also looks forward into the future, searching for
the Spirit's guidance[1].

A truly remarkable debate about the nature of Canon Law has raged
in the decades since the close of the Second Vatican Council. This pro-
tracted and profound discussion has revealed "an identity crisis" for
Canon Law because it involves quite basic questions about its very
nature and function.

Leading canonical scholars around the world, including Monsignor
Willy Onclin, have engaged in this lively discussion. The disagreements,
while civil and respectful, are both deep-seated and wide-ranging, and
the debated questions profound. What is Canon Law? Is it a juridical or
a theological science? What is its proper scope? Is Canon Law about the
regulation of word and sacrament, or about church-state relations? What
is canonical methodology? Are questions answered by legal reasoning
or by theological argument? Such questions go to the very identity of
Canon Law.

The debate is closely tied to the dueling ecclesiologies of the Second
Vatican Council, one of church as sacrament and communion, the other
of a juridically organized "perfect society".

"*Communio* ecclesiology" has now emerged as a superior and unified
theological vision which now dominates Catholic thinking about the
church. This theological development raised significant questions about
Canon Law. The canonical tradition contains such a residue of the old

---

[1] This is the central thesis of my book, *Canon Law as Ministry: Freedom and Good
Order for the Church* (New York: Paulist Press, 2000).

"perfect society" thought and content that it sometimes seems ill-suited to this post-conciliar vision of the church. Many canonical provisions crafted soon after the Council did not incorporate the more authentic theological vision which eventually emerged[2].

The kernel of my argument is that Canon Law is primarily a ministry in the church. It is a specialization within ministry, and finds its identity within the communion called church. Canon Law is a species or subset within the genus of ecclesial ministry, not a species within the genus of law or lawyering.

Canon Law is a vital ministry in the life of the church's communities and their members. Canon Law is also an academic discipline, an ancient tradition, and even a sacred science. But what is essential to grasp and hold is that Canon Law's primary identity is that of a church ministry. As a ministry Canon Law is grounded in theology, yet adapted to the pastoral needs of God's people in specific places and times, under the guidance of God's Spirit. Canon Law stands for the freedom of the faithful and strives for good order in their communities as it embodies Christ's authority as service.

If canonists are to serve the church well, we must look to the future as well as to the past. Present needs indicate several agenda items to which canonists must urgently attend. The following are examples, very important examples, of the kind of issues that the ministry of Canon Law must address. The issues are: 1) a process for revising the canons, 2) provision for diversity of discipline, and 3) the exercise of authority by women.

1. ONGOING REVISION OF THE CODES

Official Recognition of the Need

The church has long recognized the need for periodic changes in its rules of discipline, which in this era are principally expressed in its codes of canons[3], but it lacks a systematic procedure for their orderly revision.

---

[2] For example, the 1983 *Code* ascribes to the papal office the authority of a virtually absolute monarch (c. 333) while affording minimal functional expression for the college of bishops (cc. 336-339).

[3] In the twentieth century: the 1917 *Code of Canon Law*, the 1983 *Code of Canon Law*, and the 1990 *Code of Canons for the Eastern Churches*.

Before the twentieth century the church's rules were found in *collections* of canons, rather than *codes* of canons. When changes were called for, papal decrees or canons from councils were simply added to the existing collections or compiled into a new collection. It was not a tidy system. There were frequent disputes about which rule was the *ius vigens*. Still there was plenty of room for changes in the rules.

When the 1917 *Code* went into effect Pope Benedict XV made very specific provisions for its amendment:

> When in the course of time the good of the universal church calls for a new general decree ... after the decree is approved by the Pontiff, it shall be given to the Sacred Congregation of the Council [which had been created to interpret the canons of the Council of Trent], which shall reduce the decision of the decree to a canon or canons. If the decree differs from a prescription of the Code, the Council will indicate for which law of the Code the new law will substitute; if the decree treats of something about which the Code is silent, the Council will establish where the new canon or canons will be inserted into the Code, repeating the number of the preceding canon with *bis*, *ter*, etc., ... lest the numerical series be disturbed in any way[4].

This carefully crafted and detailed provision for keeping the 1917 *Code* up to date was never used[5]. Rather than make changes in the canons when new pastoral situations arose, the popes and the agencies of the Roman Curia created supplemental rules outside of the *Code*. This caused the *Code* itself to become outdated, and was one of the reasons that Pope John XXIII called for its *aggiornamento* in 1959.

The preface to the 1983 *Code* also acknowledged that there would be need for changes:

> When on account of the excessively swift changes in contemporary society certain elements of the present law become less perfect and again require a new *recognitio* (re-understanding), the church is endowed with such a wealth of resources that ... it will be able readily to undertake the renewal of the laws of its life[6].

---

[4] *Motu proprio Cum iuris canonici*, September 15, 1917, III; printed in the front of the 1917 *Code*. This same document invested Roman congregations with a "certain right of initiative in the legislative domain" which permitted them to draw up general decrees for the pope's approval. W. ONCLIN, "The Church Society and the Organization of Its Powers", *Jurist* 27(1967)3-4.

[5] When Pope Pius XII modified canon 1099 on the canonical form of marriage in 1948, it was noted in the *Code* with an asterisk and a footnote. *Motu proprio Abrogatur alterum*, August 1, 1948 (*AAS* 40(1948)305-306).

[6] Final paragraph of the unsigned preface to the 1983 *Code*.

But in 1983 no *procedure* was provided by which to make the required changes in the canons.

The 1990 *Code of Canon of the Eastern Churches* also contained a reference to the need for changes, mainly for ecumenical reasons:

> ... it is necessary that the canons of the code of the Eastern Catholic churches have the same firmness as the laws of the code of Canon Law of the Latin Church; that is, they will be in force until abrogated or changed by the supreme authority of the Church for a just cause, of which causes full communion of all of the Eastern Churches with the Catholic Church is indeed the most serious, ...[7]

Again, no process was proposed to carry out needed revisions of the canons.

In sum, the supreme legislative authority has provided no orderly and predictable way to initiate changes in the church's universal canons even though it acknowledges that Canon Law, like all systems of rules, is mutable and does in fact change.

Absence of a Process Causes Grave Harm to the Church

This lack of any orderly legislative updating process harms the Church in several ways. Most seriously, it allows serious pastoral crises to languish unattended, for example, the priest shortage, the limitations on the ministry of women, the disuse of the sacrament of penance, and the pastoral care of the divorced and remarried. The absence of a regular rule-changing process permits these critical issues to go without timely attention, sometimes for decades. It is the Christian faithful who suffer from the failure to address such disciplinary questions.

The want of an operative rule-amending procedure creates the false impression that the canons are permanent and timeless. It communicates a sense that the present rules are perfect and beyond any need for modification or improvement. And this in turn leads to canonical sclerosis. Without any reasonable expectation of change, the canons calcify, and with them the canonical ministry. Both the canons and canonists tend to decline into formalism. They become anachronistic and increasingly irrelevant. This occurred in the decades after the 1917 *Code*, and it is happening again now.

---

[7] John Paul II, Apostolic constitution *Sacri canones,* which promulgated the *CCEO*, October 18, 1990, seventh paragraph.

Another result of the absence of any procedure to respond when "certain elements of the present law become less perfect" is that the Roman Curia issues more and more instructions, declarations, and interpretations. Supplemental rules and rulings proliferate outside of the *Codes*. This too happened after 1917, and is occurring again. The Curia, even though it does not possess legislative authority, churns out a steady stream of documents containing new norms[8]. The effect is to encumber and obscure the canons with various executive "instructions" on how the rules are to be understood and applied, rather than to permit the updating and modification of the canons themselves.

There is no question that the canonical system, like any other human system of rules, needs stability. *Stabilitas legis* is indeed a high value[9]. The churches deserve firm and predictable rules by which to live. But the churches are living and active human communities, led by the Spirit of God. They grow and change, and they require an orderly process for amending, improving, and updating the rules according to which they live.

It is both anomalous and absurd for any government, state, organization, or society not to have in place an orderly and well known process for updating its rules of operation, especially given "the excessively swift changes in contemporary society". The Roman Catholic Church is no exception.

The Process Must Be Collegial

There is a pressing need for an ordinary, orderly way of amending the canons, and the procedure must be participative. Otherwise it betrays the collegial nature of the supreme authority in the Church.

The present practice by which the pope, acting alone as sole and supreme legislator, can and does take unilateral action, without any consultation of the college of bishops, to change or add to universal laws, reflects a pre-conciliar vision of papal absolutism[10].

---

[8] The scope of this proliferation is considerable. Volume VIII of *Leges Ecclesiae post Codicem Iuris Canonici Editae* was published in 1998 (Rome: EDIURCLA). It contains the "laws" issued by the Pontiff or the Curia in the ten years 1986-1995. It is a book of 1500 double-columned pages of fine print containing excerpts from 456 documents.

[9] Stability or relative permanence does not imply that canonical rules should not change. Indeed the common good sometimes requires temporary legal provisions. W. ONCLIN, "La Nocion de Ley Canonica", *Ius Canonicum* 7(1967)38-40.

[10] The one legislative change in the canons since the promulgation of the 1983 and 1990 *Codes* illustrates the lack of a collegial amendment process. The apostolic letter *Ad*

This practice profoundly contradicts the Church's own theological identity. It defies the synodal and conciliar patterns for rule-making which have been the revered and preferred tradition in the church since the "Council of Jerusalem" in Acts 15[11].

Both the Second Vatican Council and the *Codes* affirm that the college of bishops also possesses supreme and full power over the universal church along with the pope[12]. One form of that authority is legislative. But there is presently no practical way for the college to exercise its legitimate lawmaking power. The college of bishops can change canonical rules when acting in an ecumenical council[13], but such councils are rare, cumbersome, and difficult.

Episcopal Synods Could Provide a Structure

The college of bishops could collaborate with the pope in revising canonical rules in the context of episcopal synods. The synodal structure already exists, and, when it meets in general session it is broadly representative of the entire college. However, at present episcopal synods are merely consultative gatherings, purely advisory to the pope and completely controlled by his authority[14]. Moreover, as they presently function the synodal events are effectively stifled by the heavy representation of curial officials.

But synods are capable of acting deliberatively, if and when the pope gives them that power[15]. The popes have not entrusted the synods with issues to decide formally since they first began meeting in 1967. The result of a synod's deliberations would still require papal ratification in order to have binding force, so if and when they were given rule-making authority there would be no threat to papal primacy.

---

tuendam fidem (May 18, 1998) added sections to canons 751 and 1371 of the Latin *Code* and 598 and 1436 of the Eastern *Code*. It did so *motu proprio*, by a single, solitary action of the supreme pontiff, without any consultation of the college of bishops, solely at the behest of the Congregation for the Doctrine of Faith. The "*collegial* spirit" which the apostolic constitution *Sacrae disciplinae leges* (January 25, 1983) extolled ("it corresponds perfectly with the teaching and character of the Second Vatican Council") was entirely absent from this legislative action. (The sad truth is that this mode of lawmaking resembles the style of an absolute monarch or dictator more than it does the rule-making process described in the Acts of the Apostles, 15.)

[11] Confer *La Synodalité: La participation au gouvernement dans l'Église*, two-volume issue of *L'Année Canonique*, the acts of the seventh international congress of Canon Law, Paris, September, 1990 (Paris: Letouzey et Ané, 1992).

[12] *LG* 22; *CIC*, c. 336; *CCEO*, c. 49.

[13] *CIC*, cc. 337, 338.

[14] *CIC*, cc. 342, 344.

[15] *CIC*, c. 343.

The structure of synods should be altered to make of them more effective instruments of collegial governance, but even under the present rules there is nothing to prevent episcopal synods from meeting in legislative sessions. Proposed canonical changes could be circulated well in advance of synodal sessions[16]. The bishops and the pope together could consider and discuss suggested alterations in the canons, and in this way, legislate in collaboration, in a truly collegial manner. The Church's *Codes* of canons could be kept current in a regularly occurring and reasonable way.

The need for a reasonable legislative process is urgent.

2. REGIONAL DIVERSITY OF DISCIPLINE

Regional diversity of discipline within particular and local churches of the Catholic communion has been a reality for many centuries. Indeed, diversity and not uniformity was the dominant and persistent pattern of church life from the very beginning and throughout history. The great canonical collections of the past both revealed that diversity and helped to keep it harmonious[17]. In more recent centuries the exercise of papal authority in a centralizing direction has gradually constricted diversity of discipline in the church. The twentieth century codifications of uniform discipline for the "church universal" are real innovations within the rich Catholic tradition. Compare this present trend toward uniformity with times past.

A History of Diversity

The New Testament churches successfully bridged the gap between Jewish and Gentile practices without suppressing either. This tension between different traditions was resolved in the "Council of Jerusalem". "It is the decision of the Holy Spirit, and ours too, not to lay on you any burden beyond that which is strictly necessary[18]." In other words, minimal restrictions were imposed and maximum respect was given for the differing practices. In those first decades these churches also made

---

[16] As the *lineamenta* and *instrumenta laboris* are now sent out months in advance, permitting extensive study and consultations in all part of the Church.

[17] Recall the title of John Gratian's epoch-making collection: *Concordia Discordantium Canonum* ("a harmony of discordant canons"; ca.1140).

[18] Acts 15, 28; see also Gal 2.

themselves at home in both Semitic and Graeco-Roman cultures. The diversity of their internal ministries is well known[19].

The "church of the Empire" (the fourth century and afterward) was far from uniform, even long after it was supported by imperial authority and law. Local church communities grew and thrived among all of the various peoples around the Mediterranean basin who were subjects of that imperial authority. The differences in their practices were debated and resolved in the earliest church councils[20].

Throughout the fifth to eighth centuries the Christian movement encountered and evangelized the peoples who invaded the crumbling Empire or lived on its outer fringes. The churches which took root among the Franks, Visigoths, Vandals, Lombards, and Celts all assumed elements from those cultures and were likewise influenced by them.

The later European missionary efforts of the ninth to eleventh centuries, which reached the Polish and Slavic peoples, the Magyars, Bohemians, and Scandinavians, established local churches which incorporated customs and practices of these peoples. Sometimes there were disputes about which "pagan" practices could be reconciled with the Christian faith, but settlements were reached and the local communities were accepted in communion.

The missionary efforts of the sixteenth and seventeenth centuries attempted to found churches in the "new worlds" of Africa, America, and Asia. In some places, e.g., China, Japan, and India, these heroic efforts were frustrated by the inability or unwillingness, on the part of the missionaries or their Roman superiors, to adapt to the cultures and languages of the indigenous peoples. In other places, e.g., Central and South America, the Philippines, and Goa, the new churches thrived, but often in modalities that were distinctly European rather than indigenous.

A World Church

At the outset of the twenty-first century, regional Catholic churches all over the earth recognize themselves as integral components of a "world church". They are conscious of the need "to inculturate", that is, to relate reciprocally to their various cultures, while remaining one worldwide communion. They know that they must make the Gospel incarnate in their own culture while at the same time introducing the

---

[19] Confer, for example, the diverse leadership structures mentioned in 1 Cor 12, 28, Eph 4, 11, 1Tim 3, Titus 1.

[20] E.g., the canons of the Councils of Nicaea (a. 325) and Chalcedon (a. 451).

people around them, together with their positive cultural practices, into the local church communities.

Diversity of discipline is a fact of the church's history and present reality. The variety of practices represented in this healthy diversity go much deeper than mere superficial differences in liturgical vestments, sacred music, or church architecture. It includes different ways of baptizing and anointing, different forms of receiving Holy Communion, clerical marriage and clerical celibacy, election of bishops and appointment of bishops, permanent pastors and temporary pastors, personal parishes as well as territorial ones. It is clear that a considerable diversity of discipline among the churches existed from the beginnings of the Christian tradition, and still exists today, despite the strong tendencies toward imposing uniformity.

Beyond recognizing the fact of diversity and its full legitimacy, inculturation calls for the ability to continue to adapt church practices so that they are meaningful to people in particular places and times, so that the people see them as their own and not as something foreign to them. Of course, the adaptations to various cultures must always be in keeping with the common faith and not jeopardize the strong bonds of communion. However, genuine inculturation demands a healthy diversity of practice.

Subsidiarity and Diversity

Subsidiarity implies an appropriate autonomy and self-direction for regional as well as ritual churches. These regional embodiments are always committed to the communion of churches, those nearby, and all others within the communion of the universal church. But, these regional expressions of the church also possess their own identities, proper responsibilities, and legitimate freedom of action.

Pope Pius XI articulated the principle of subsidiarity in his landmark encyclical on the reconstruction of the social order[21]. He described it as "that most weighty principle, which cannot be set aside or changed, [and which] remains fixed and unshaken in social philosophy":

> Just as it is gravely wrong to take from individuals what they can accomplish by their own initiative and industry and give it to the community, so

---

[21] *Quadragesimo anno*, Encyclical Letter on the Fortieth Anniversary of *Rerum novarum*, May 15, 1931; *AAS* 23(1931)177-228; *Proclaiming Justice and Peace*, M. WALSH & B. DAVIES, eds. (Mystic, CN: Twenty-Third Publications, 1991)41-80.

also it is an injustice and at the same time a grave evil and disturbance of
right order to assign to a greater and higher association what lesser and
subordinate organizations can do. For every social activity ought of its very
nature to furnish help to the members of the body social, and never destroy
and absorb them (QA 79).

Pope John XXIII repeated the definition in *Mater et magistra*[22] and
called it the "guiding principle of subsidiary function" (*MM* 53). Pope
John Paul II restated the principle again in 1991[23]:

Here again the principle of subsidiarity must be respected. A community
of a higher order should not interfere in the internal life of a community
of a lower order, depriving the latter of its functions, but rather should
support it in case of need and help to coordinate its activity with the
activities of the rest of society, always with a view to the common good
(*CA* 48).

The application of this principle *within the church*, as well as within
the larger society, has been repeatedly affirmed by the church's own
authorities[24]. In 1967 the principle of subsidiarity was formally
adopted by the Synod of Bishops as one of the principles to guide the
revision of the Code of Canon Law: "Careful attention is to be given
to the greater application of the principle of subsidiarity within the
Church[25]."

What does the principle of subsidiarity mean for regional churches? It
affirms a healthy legitimate autonomy of regional groupings of churches

---

[22] Encyclical Letter on a Reevaluation of the Social Question, May 15, 1961; *AAS*
53(1961)401-464; *Proclaiming Justice and Peace*, 81-124.

[23] *Centesimus annus*, Encyclical Letter on the One Hundredth Anniversary of *Rerum
novarum*, May 1, 1991; *AAS* 83(1991)854; *Proclaiming Justice and Peace*, 432-478.

[24] In addresses by Pope Pius XII on Feb. 20, 1946 (*AAS* 38(1946)145), and by Pope
Paul VI on Oct. 27, 1969 (*AAS* 61(1969)729).

[25] Principle No. 5, quoted in the Preface to the 1983 *Code of Canon Law*. The much
fuller text of the principle of subsidiarity that was to govern the *Code*'s revision is found
in *Communicationes* 1(1969)80-82; it twice mentions regional provisions. W. Onclin
described the principle of subsidiarity as one of the principal "lines of force" of the new
Code. "Le Nouveau Code de Droit Canonique", *Ephemerides Theologicae Lovanienses*
60(1984)339-340.

The sudden and shocking suggestion, made by the Secretary of the Congregation of
the Doctrine of the Faith on the eve of the 1985 Synod of Bishops, to call into question
the application of the principle of subsidiarity within the church has been sharply chal-
lenged. Confer A. LEYS, *Ecclesiological Impacts of the Principle of Subsidiarity* (Kampen: Uitgeverij Kok, 1995), R. HARRINGTON, *The Applicability of the Principle of Subsidiarity According to the Code of Canon Law* (Ottawa: St. Paul University, 1997;
doctoral dissertation), and J. BURKHARD, "The Interpretation and Application of Subsidiarity in Ecclesiology: An Overview of the Theological and Canonical Literature",
Jurist (forthcoming).

within the universal communion. It encourages decision-making and adaptation within the general norms of the church. Such legitimate regional adaptation should be fostered and facilitated, rather than hobbled and hindered. Subsidiarity does not imply complete autonomy, much less independence, from the supreme collegial authority of the church's governance.

Conciliar Protection and Promotion of Diversity

The salient question is, how is this regional diversity of discipline going to be maintained and develop? How can it be fostered and monitored? The answer lies in the church's tradition of conciliar structures.

During the early centuries a rich variety of regional disciplinary practices was established and maintained through regional synods, for instance, in North Africa, in southern France, in central Spain[26], as well as by the established synods of the patriarchal churches: Antioch, Alexandria, Jerusalem, and Constantinople. These decisional and policy-making bodies exercised real authority in their regions both before and since papal primacy was acknowledged and papal decretal activity became prevalent.

Regional councils functioned throughout the Merovingian (sixth and seventh centuries) and the Carolingian (eighth and ninth centuries) periods. This pattern of regional conciliar action evolved into the system of provincial and metropolitan councils which continued throughout the middles ages.

As papal authority waxed in modern times, regional conciliar activity waned[27]. Roman authority became stronger and more centralized, and it gradually resisted and broke down the pattern of conciliar functioning.

Sometimes the decrees of the popes and the directives of their curial congregations recognize and respect regional differences. At their best they safeguard regional and ritual traditions, and even encourage local adaptations. However, their dominant tendency, over the centuries, is toward centralized decision-making and uniform practices. Obviously, this trend operates to the detriment of regional decision-making and local adaptations.

---

[26] More than twenty such regional synods were held in the fourth century alone, in places like Carthage, Arles, and Toledo.

[27] The provincial and plenary councils of Baltimore bear ample witness to the enduring effectiveness and influence of conciliar activity in the United States throughout the nineteenth century; it ceased completely in the twentieth.

Restrictions on Regional Conciliarity

There are at least four manifestations of conciliar decision-making at regional levels:
1) synods of bishops meeting in special session for a given region, e.g., the recent episcopal synods for Europe, Africa, Asia, and America[28], 2) plenary councils for all of the dioceses whose bishops belong to the same conference of bishops[29], 3) provincial councils for the various dioceses of the same ecclesiastical province[30], and 4) conferences of bishops of a given nation or territory.

However, in the twentieth century Roman authorities have insisted on increasing levels of control over all four of these forums, especially when it comes to making rules. Episcopal synods could resolve issues and issue decrees, but that deliberative authority has not been given to them[31]. Plenary councils cannot be held without the prior permission of the Apostolic See, and the norms which both plenary and provincial councils decide upon cannot be promulgated until the Holy See has approved them[32]. These severe restrictions constitute one reason why such particular councils no longer occur. Parallel limitations severely confine the rule-making activity of episcopal conferences[33]. Their decrees require a two-thirds majority, an usually stringent standard. Then the pre-promulgation review (*recognitio*) of conference decisions by the Apostolic See further restricts conference rule-making activity and consequently obstructs the healthy processes of innovation and adaptation[34].

This effective suppression of regional self-determination leaves the universal norms of the codes in virtually exclusive control, that is, with a near monopoly on ecclesial discipline, even in matters of fine detail.

---

[28] *CIC*, c. 345.

[29] *CIC*, c. 439.

[30] *CIC*, c. 440.

[31] *CIC*, c. 343.

[32] *CIC* cc. 439, 446; 1917 *CIC*, c. 291.1. The source for the requirement to have the acts and decrees of plenary and provincial councils approved by the Holy See stems from a 1893 letter of the Propagation of the Faith to the East Indies (*CIC Fontes* VII, n. 4928).

[33] Confer *CIC* c. 455. The 1983 *Code* requires or allows episcopal conferences to make applications of general norms to the churches of their conference. These "complementary norms" or "particular legislation" are called for in forty-three specific instances. Confer J.T. MARTÍN DE AGAR, *Legislazione delle Conferenze Episcopali Complementare al C.I.C.* (Milano: Giuffrè, 1990).

[34] *CIC*, c. 455.2. The agencies of the Apostolic See frequently reject or amend norms proposed by bishops' conferences, a practice which both humiliates them and frustrates their efforts to fashion suitable regional applications.

The whole process is centripetal, directed toward the center. It not only restricts legislative power to the central authority, but it persistently compels uniformity of practice to the detriment of cultural and pastoral adaptation.

In sum, uniform universal legislation, epitomized in the canonical codes of the twentieth century and enforced by the supreme central authority, has replaced the long tradition of regional adaptation. The post-conciliar promise of a return to collegiality and subsidiary function have failed to materialize. As a result, the Roman Catholic communion lacks the means for effective regional self-regulation and pastoral adaptation.

As noted above, the unity of the entire Catholic communion is essential. But it is a unity in essentials (*in necessariis*), and freedom is to be encouraged in all other matters, including various forms of discipline (*in variis formis ... disciplinae*)[35]. This legitimate diversity of discipline is also a high value. Ultimately, the Holy Spirit is the guarantor of the church's unity as well as the impetus behind its diversity. "Do not stifle the Spirit[36]."

3. WOMEN AND THE EXERCISE OF AUTHORITY

Prominence of Women in Ministry

Recent trends in the United States provide an example of this phenomenon. More lay ministers than priests now staff parishes in the United States. There are about nineteen thousand parishes in the U.S. As of 1997 they are served by just over 27,000 priests and just over 29,000 lay persons. Eighty-two percent of these paid, professional ministers are women, 29% religious and 71% lay women[37]. The trend toward more women in parish ministry continues, and it is increasingly obvious.

What is somewhat less obvious is the number and influence of women in ministry at the diocesan level. There are 192 dioceses in the U.S. In 1994 from 25 to 60 percent of diocesan professional staff positions were filled by women, depending on the level of staff responsibility[38]. The numbers are in the hundreds rather than thousands, but these are leader-

---

[35] *UR*, 4.

[36] 1 Thes 5, 19.

[37] P. MURNION & D. DELAMBO, *Parishes and Parish Ministers: A Study of Parish Lay Ministry* (New York: National Pastoral Life Center, 1999) p. iii.

[38] M. CARNEY, "Current Pastoral Practice", *Creating A Home: Benchmarks for Church Leadership Roles for Women* (Silver Spring, MD: Leadership Conference of Women Religious, 1996)70-73.

ship roles, not secretarial or support staff positions. Another survey in 1996 reported that in many dioceses the clear majority of ministry is being performed by women[39].

In spite of this increasing prominence of women in very responsible ecclesial offices, their canonical recognition and empowerment continues to be minimal.

Official Encouragement for the Inclusion of Women

The Second Vatican Council affirmed the basic equality between men and women, and went on to urge ever greater recognition of that equality and to condemn discrimination based on gender[40].

The 1987 Synod of Bishops "On the Vocation and Mission of the Laity in the Church and in the World" advanced the propositions that:

> The church must recognize all the gifts of men and women for its life and mission, and put them into practice.
> In the life of the church women should also be participants without discrimination in giving advice and reaching decisions[41].

The apostolic exhortation on the laity which followed from that Synod urged the same themes:

> In speaking about participation in the apostolic mission of the church, there is no doubt that in virtue of baptism and confirmation, a woman – as well as a man – is made a sharer in the threefold mission of Jesus Christ, priest, prophet and king, and is thereby charged and given the ability to fulfill the fundamental apostolate of the church: evangelization.

As Paul VI has already said ... "we can recognize and promote the role of women in the mission of evangelization and in the life of the Christian community." Above all, the acknowledgment in theory of the active and responsible presence of women in the church must be realized in practice[42].

---

[39] "The high degree of involvement by women in the life of the diocese was attested to be a significant number of respondents. One bishop stated that 80% of all ecclesial ministry in his diocese was done by women. Another bishop identified it as 90%. Several others referred simply to the vast majority of ministry being done by women." R. SMITH, "*Strengthening the Bonds of Peace* Revisited", *Canon Law Society of America Proceedings* 58(1996)366.

[40] *LG* 32; *GS* 29.

[41] Propositions 46.1 and 47.5 (*Origins* 17:29(Dec. 31, 1987)508).

[42] John Paul II, *Christifideles laici*, Dec. 30, 1988, par. 51 (*Origins* 18:35 (Feb. 9, 1989)586).

In 1994 the National Conference of Catholic Bishops in the U.S. stated:

> We welcome this leadership [of women], ... and we commit ourselves to enhancing the participation of women in every possible aspect of church life.
>
> An important issue for women is how to have a voice in the governance of the church to which they belong and which they serve with love and generosity. This can be achieved in at least two ways: through consultation and through cooperation in the exercise of authority.
>
> This may be a graced moment in the life of the church which enables us to take a fresh and deeper look at the relationship between jurisdiction and ordained ministry, and thus gain a better understanding of legislative, executive and judicial acts within the church[43].

Both the 1983 *Code* and the 1990 Eastern *Code* repeat the conciliar teaching on equality, but both fail to recognize and facilitate that equality fully[44].

The Need and Possibility for Empowerment

The ample and expert service of women in the church is welcome and increasingly acknowledged, but these women ministers are still perceived to be in subservient roles in a male-dominated church[45]. Their able and legitimate leadership needs to be publicly authenticated; they need to be fully included in policy-forming and decision-making. In short, for the good of the whole church women need to be empowered within it.

Heretofore, conflicting theories about the source of authority in the church limited lay persons to a "sharing in" or "cooperating in" the power of governance which really *belonged* only to the ordained. These polarized positions on the source of authority in the church have now been transcended by a theology of lay participation which relies on the sacraments of initiation, the power and gifts of the Holy Spirit,

---

[43] Pastoral reflection, *Strengthening the Bonds of Peace* Nov. 16, 1994 (*Origins* 24:25 (Dec. 1, 1994)419-420).

[44] E.g., *CIC*, cc. 208, 606; *CCEO*, c. 11. But lay persons may only "cooperate in the exercise of the power of governance" whereas those in sacred orders "are capable of the power of governance" (*CIC*, c. 129; *CCEO*, c. 979).

[45] R. WALLACE, "Catholic Women and the Creation of a New Social Reality", *Gender & Society* 2:1(March, 1988)24-38.

and full communion which carries with it a real share in Christ's teaching, sanctifying, and ruling functions[46].

This persuasive theological development clears the way for the canons to catch up with life. Canonical discipline can and should recognize the full reality of what is actually happening "on the ground", namely that thousands of lay women and men have been and presently are exercising the power of governance. They are not only capable and qualified for the power of governance (*habiles potestatis regiminis*), they actually possess and exercise that power in the church every day.

Recommended Changes in the Canons

Lay members of the Christian faithful, women as well as men, should be accorded the canonical levels of participation in the church's governance to which their theological status and ministerial responsibilities entitles them.

In order to bring canonical rules into greater agreement with both theological theory and accepted practice, at least these alterations in the 1983 *Code* need to be made:

C. 129.2

From: Lay members of the Christian faithful can cooperate in the exercise of this same power according to the norm of law.
To: Lay members of the Christian faithful are also qualified (*habiles*) for the power of governance according to the norm of law.

C. 274.1

From: Only clerics can obtain offices for whose exercise the power of orders or the power of ecclesiastical governance is required.
To: Only clerics can obtain offices for whose exercise the power of orders is required.

---

[46] Confer the sources cited in the concluding section of J. BEAL, "The Exercise of the Power of Governance by Lay People: State of the Question", *Jurist* 55(1995)85-92. W. Onclin recognized that the three functions of governmental power - legislative, administrative, and judicial - can be accomplished by those to whom the supreme authority or bishops confide the exercise of the functions. "The Church Society", *Jurist* 27(1967)14. He saw no obstacle, aside from the positive law provision of 1917 *CIC*, c. 118, which limited the power of jurisdiction to clerics, to communities of the faithful participating in the exercise of legislative power. "La Nocion de Ley Canonica", *Ius Canonicum* 7(1967)30.

C. 473.2

From: Where it is expedient, a moderator of the curia may be appointed who must be a priest and who, under the authority of the bishop, is to coordinate those things which pertain to the treatment of administrative affairs ...

To: Where it is expedient, a moderator of the curia may be appointed who, under the authority of the bishop, is to coordinate ...

C. 478.1

From: A vicar general and an episcopal vicar are to be priests not less than thirty years old, doctors or licensed in canon law or theology or at least truly expert in these disciplines, ...

To: A vicar general and an episcopal vicar are to be not less than thirty years old, doctors or licensed in canon law or theology ...

C. 546

From: To be appointed a parochial vicar, one must be in the sacred order of the presbyterate.

To: To be appointed a parochial vicar, one must be in the sacred order of the presbyterate or the diaconate or otherwise qualified to exercise the office.

C. 564

From: A chaplain is a priest to whom is entrusted in a stable manner the pastoral care, at least in part, of some community or particular group of the Christian faithful, ...

To: A chaplain is a priest, deacon, or other member of the Christian faithful to whom is entrusted in a stable manner the pastoral care, at least in part, of some community ...

C. 1420.4

From: Both the judicial vicar and the adjutant judicial vicars must be priests, of unimpaired reputation, doctors or at least licensed in canon law ...

To: Both the judicial vicar and the adjutant judicial vicars must be priests, deacons, or other members of the Christian faithful, of unimpaired reputation, doctors or at least licensed ...

C. 1421.1

From: In a diocese, the bishop is to appoint diocesan judges, who are to be clerics.

To: In a diocese, the bishop is to appoint diocesan judges, who are to be priests, deacons, or other members of the Christian faithful.

These few changes in the church's canons would accord appropriate juridical recognition to the true dignity and rightful participation of lay persons in the church's life. They would clear the canonical path so that qualified lay persons, women and men, could both possess the power of governance as well as exercise it. Lay persons could be officially named to offices which they actually fill, but which are presently closed to them canonically[47].

Several other disciplinary issues stand out on the canonical "urgent reform agenda", for instance: the ordination of married men to the priesthood in the Western church, the acknowledgment of the right and duty of everyone of the faithful to exercise the gifts of the Spirit for the upbuilding of the church (*AA* 3), the canonical rights and obligations of parishes and other local communities of the faithful, and better provisions for ecumenical progress[48].

"GOVERNING IN LOVE"

Article two of the Decree on Ecumenism (*Unitatis Redintegratio*) reveals a vision of church governance which canonists should cherish and follow. The entire passage about the bonds of unity in the church is of surpassing theological power and beauty. The Holy Spirit is everywhere: calling, gathering together, dwelling within, ruling over, bringing about communion, distributing graces and offices, enriching the church with different functions "in order to equip the saints for the work of service, so as to build up the body of Christ". (Ephes 4, 12).

The tasks entrusted to the college of the twelve and their successors, under the action of the Spirit, include preaching of the gospel, administration of the sacraments, and *governing the church in love* (*per gubernationem in dilectione*). By exercising authority with love, the church's leaders are to perfect the communion of Christ's people in unity, and to

---

[47] Some other canons which discriminate on the basis of gender should also be altered, e.g., *CIC*, c. 602, which describes the life of sisters as *vita fraterna*, c. 667, which requires the papal cloister only for monasteries of nuns, and c. 1089, which limits the marriage impediment of abduction to women.

[48] W. Onclin, during the *Code* revision process, stated that canon law must be at the service of the charismatic church, it must promote the more perfect realization of the communion of faith and charity, and should avoid "anything which could be harmful to ecumenical action". "Church and Church Law", *Theological Studies* 28(1967)745.

maintain the harmony of God's family (*concordia in familia Dei*). If they do so, then the pilgrim church can hope to be a sign lifted high for the nations to see, ministering a gospel of peace to all humankind.

We canonists must find the meaning of "governing in love" for ourselves, even as we strive for canonical reform. It must mean more than encountering people politely, more than doing justice with a smile. Governing in love means ministering with loving care, the kind of loving care we hope our own family members receive when they need ministry. And governing in love means seeking to increase love as a result of our ministry, not love for us, but love among the members of our faithful communities, and love for the One who demonstrated God's unconditional love for us[49].

---

[49] See B. GRIFFIN, "The Challenge of Ecumenism for Canonists", *Canon Law Society of America Proceedings* 55(1993)32-38.

FULL-TIME PASTORAL MINISTERS AND DIOCESAN GOVERNANCE

Roch Pagé

PRELIMINARY REMARKS

It is indeed a great privilege and honour for me to be part of the "Monsignor W. Onclin Chair 2001" activities, and I wish to thank most heartily Professor Rik Torfs, Dean of the Faculty of Canon Law, and the authorities of the Catholic University of Leuven for their kind invitation and most gracious hospitality. For a number of years now, I have been aware of the activities of the Onclin Chair and have appreciated the annual publications. I must admit, though, that I never dreamed that one day I would be here as an invited guest. Furthermore, it is a particular honour for me to be able to share this week with my friend and colleague of many years, Father James Coriden. The programme you have developed is an outstanding example of inter-institutional cooperation and it can readily serve as a model for others. You have certainly found an appropriate way to honour the memory of one of the most outstanding canonists of our time, Monsignor William Onclin and deserve congratulations for your untiring efforts to promote collaboration and the sharing of ideas.

Today, I would like to share some thoughts with you regarding a topic that is close to my heart. I do not think for a moment, though, that I am presenting the final word on the matter, since the matter is still relatively new. It would not be the appropriate time to establish definitive rules and regulations, as is also the case for the so-called "new" ministries. We do not yet have enough experience in these areas. In spite of this limitation, I would like to raise some questions in the light of current pastoral experiences in Canada and elsewhere. I would propose, then, first of all, to set a context, then draw attention to a number of observations relating to this context. From there, I would consider certain issues referring more directly to the power of governance, and, finally, make a proposal that people might wish to consider and, with time, debate and refine.

I. THE CONTEXT

Baptism and confirmation have come a long way since the time when they were considered simply as means of constituting the laity into the "taught Church", as distinct from the bishops who were the "teaching Church." Although they were the basis for lay involvement *in the world* at the time when *Catholic Action* was being promoted, baptism and confirmation are today seen as the foundation of the laity's participation in the very exercise of ministry *within the Church*. In former times, no apostolate carried out under the banner of *Catholic Action* could be legitimately exercised without a "mandate from the hierarchy", as it was then called. It is somewhat the same today with the new types of lay involvement in the Church, although the basis is notably different. The bishop's mandate now "authorizes"; it allows a lay person either to exercise officially a ministry in the Church or to participate in the exercise of a ministry. In the past, when we spoke of "the apostolate of the laity", we referred to "involved" lay persons and we knew that it meant that their involvement was *in the world*. Yet, at the same time as they are involved in pastoral activities, the laity are also "employed" if their qualities and qualifications conform to the conditions set out in job descriptions and if they have a contract similar to employees in secular enterprises. They no longer are said to exercise their action in the world but rather within ecclesial structures. For this reason, today, we prefer to speak of "lay ministries" or of "lay pastoral ministers", and, not surprisingly, the term "apostolate" is used less frequently and has been replaced by "pastoral ministry". Of course, I am aware of the reservations about the use of the term "ministry" expressed in the 1997 Interdicasterial Instruction on the collaboration of the non-ordained faithful in the ministry of priests, but I am using the term here in a more general sense.

I intentionally used the word "full-time" in the title of this presentation instead of "permanent", despite its being the generally accepted term, especially in French-speaking areas where we refer to *Agents pastoraux permanents* or "Permanent Pastoral Workers". I prefer the term "full-time" because even if the theological foundation – baptism – is permanent, the exercise of lay ministry depends on a juridical act, the granting of the mandate. Lay persons work full-time for the duration of their mandate, but this does not make them ministers or permanent workers.

Therefore, I prefer to reserve the term "permanent" for ordained ministers, precisely because they are ordained to ministry, or, if you prefer, because they receive sacred Orders for ministry. They are empowered to undertake this ministry in the name of Christ and of the Church. Baptism and confirmation do not do this. Furthermore, even if clerics are permanent because of their ordination, they still need a mandate to exercise their ministry in a given office. But they are permanent ministers, which is not the case with lay persons. Likewise, although permanent deacons do not always exercise their ministry full-time, they are still permanent.

This being said, might it be possible to read canon 274, §1 in a new light? "Only clerics can obtain those offices for whose exercise is required the power of orders or the power of ecclesiastical governance." As we know, the interpretation of this canon is somewhat problematic. Is the canon referring to a radical *possibility* or only to a *right* to such offices? How is it that the laity can exercise judicial power when canon 274, §1 implies that it is the laying on of hands that qualifies a person for the exercise of the power of governance? But, no matter how the canon is interpreted, I prefer the interpretation which calls for it to be read not only according to its text but also in its context in the Code. For instance, since the canon is found in the chapter on the obligations and rights of clerics, does this mean that only clerics would have a *right* to *receive* offices involving the exercise of the power of orders or of governance? Or would this exclude lay persons from also *receiving* such offices, even if according to this interpretation, they would not have a *right* to them? The jury is still out.

Let us say then that in participating in the exercise of the pastoral office, clerics and lay persons relate more to each other in the *stability* granted to them by their mandate, than in the *permanence* which constitutes the basis of their mandate since this may vary from one person to another.

Finally, we note that there is a new tendency these days, at least in Quebec dioceses, to apply the expression "Permanent Pastoral Agents or Workers" equally to priests, permanent deacons and lay persons, as well as to religious. Their common denominators are full-time commitment and a legitimate mandate from the bishop.

II. OBSERVATIONS RELATIVE TO THE NEW CONTEXT

Before proceeding further in our analysis, a few observations must be made relating to situations in which ministry is now exercised.

A. Qualities for active involvement of the laity

The first point to make is that, regardless of the reasons which led to the full-time involvement of lay persons and their participation in the exercise of the bishop's pastoral office, it is better to presume that they are here to stay and, therefore, we should act accordingly. A bishop was once asked what he would do if he were to receive ten more priests immediately. After briefly considering the question, he replied that none of them should replace the lay persons involved full-time in various pastoral offices in his diocese. And yet, is it not true that these same lay persons were originally employed because of a shortage of priests?

But, if such were the case, we must nevertheless recognize that it is not the shortage of priests nor the bishop's mandate that provide the basis or foundation for the ministry entrusted to the laity today. The bishop's mandate merely recognizes that a lay person has the required qualities to fulfil the given office. This person does not acquire the qualities from the mandate. If the shortage of priests was the occasion for the emergence of lay persons in ecclesial structures, a return to a sufficient number of priests should not deprive lay persons of the capacity which a mandate can recognize. This situation led one bishop to ask that all the parish priests in his diocese form a pastoral team modeled on canon 517, §2, even though there was not a shortage of priests in the diocese at the time. This was done only so that lay persons could take the place which is rightfully theirs as baptized members of the Church. The bishop's document did not explicitly mention this, but, in fact, he wanted to prepare the priests and laity for the situations we are facing today.

B. The rapid growth of lay involvement

The second point to keep in mind is that the Code does not seem to have anticipated the rapid growth of lay involvement in pastoral structures. The least we can say is that it is very cautious when we compare its norms with the tasks lay persons assume in reality, whether in parishes, dioceses, teaching institutions, hospitals, or elsewhere.

This cautiousness is found in the norms regarding involvement in ministry, as well as participation in the various structures of government. Suffice it to say that in the Code, the term "pastor" or "chaplain" is never given to lay persons; rather, they are introduced in canon 228 as assistants to the "sacred pastors" and to the "pastors of the Church". At any rate, canon 225, §1 already asserted that lay persons are deputed by God to the apostolate (not to pastoral activities) "through their baptism and confirmation". We can also note the confusion surrounding the meaning of canon 129, §2 on the eventual "cooperation" of lay persons in the power of governance. How are we to reconcile this text with canon 274, §1 which appears, at least at first sight, to limit to clerics offices requiring the power of governance?

Canons 129 and 274 serve as principles, but they are probably not exhaustive. In practice, apart from the possibility of lay persons acting as judges, and this only by exception, the Code speaks of lay persons as "supplying" certain offices when there is a lack of ministers of the Word, of baptism or of communion. This same principle underlies canon 517, §2: if there is "a shortage of priests, [...] a deacon or some other person who is not a priest [... could] be entrusted with a share in the exercise of the pastoral care of a parish." There are two things to note here: the text does not say that lay persons will be entrusted with pastoral care, but rather with a "share of the exercise of the pastoral care." Furthermore, the enumeration of such persons begins with "a deacon".

What exactly is the meaning of "a shortage of priests"? This could be very relative – relative to the large number of priests of days gone by, which in many dioceses enabled bishops to erect parishes quite liberally, in fact as soon as a certain number of families would gather outside of an established parish or territory. We now question whether such a great number of parishes was really necessary. The shortage of priests might also be related to the number of priests qualified to be pastors. Not too long ago, for instance, we had the impression that most young priests felt they were called to work with youth rather than in a parish environment. Today, however, because of the numerous court cases, they are reluctant to volunteer to work with youth, or, if they do, they are often treated with suspicion. And, who knows? Maybe we had too many priests in the past.

C. The dispensing power of lay persons

No one will deny that the Code allows lay persons to participate in various ways in the exercise of the power of governance. Does this form of participation entail the power of dispensing, for example, from the diriment impediments to marriage? Several canonists believe that lay persons can indeed dispense, and they base their argument on the absence of any legislation forbidding it, and even, as a last resort, by invoking a doubt of law. Others say that they cannot do so. Midway between these opinions lies another opinion that a dispensation granted by a lay person would be valid according to canon 10 which stipulates that "only those laws which expressly state that an act is null or that a person is incapable of acting are to be considered to be invalidating or incapacitating." Be that as it may, we must not forget that something can be expressly mentioned either implicitly or explicitly. Also, and finally, resorting to this canon is somewhat of an admission that the argument in favour of the lay person's power of dispensing is on rather shaky ground.

So, as the Code now stands, I personally believe that lay persons cannot be delegated to exercise the faculty of dispensing from universal or particular law, even though they might be capable of being authorized to verify the existence of required conditions and to act on behalf of the bishop who grants the dispensation through them. But, we have to recognize there are too many opportunities in the Code where lay persons could have been explicitly mentioned to evoke a *lacuna* or an absence of legislation. One has only to consider the exhaustive list in canon 89: "Parish priests and other priests or deacons cannot dispense from universal or particular law unless this power is expressly granted to them." Lay persons are not mentioned here.

Might there be a possible exception to what I have just noted? What about the case of a lay person who has been duly delegated to assist at a marriage and who finds him or herself in the situation envisioned in canons 1079 and 1080 – an impediment of ecclesiastical law is discovered and there is danger of death, or everything has been prepared for the wedding? Despite the fact that these canons do not explicitly mention a delegated lay person, but instead refer to a delegated "sacred minister" which implies the reception of orders (c. 1008), could the delegated lay person have the power to dispense, not in virtue of the absence of legislation but because of canon 138, which stipulates that "delegation of power to a person is understood to include everything necessary for the exercise of that power"? This being the case, I would not be overly surprised if some day an official interpretation from the *Pontifical Council for the Interpretation of Legislative Texts*, or even better, a papal *Motu proprio*, concerning the legitimacy of the delegation of lay persons to exercise the power of dispensing from universal or particular law were to be issued. All in all, I have no objection in principle. I am only saying that in its actual state, the law does not seem to permit it.

This probably will influence to some extent the manner in which lay persons can "cooperate" in the exercise of the power of governance.

D. Membership of lay persons in diocesan councils

A fourth observation concerns the place of lay persons in organizations assisting the bishop in the government of his diocese. Among the mandatory organizations, not one of them must necessarily include lay persons among its members. For example, the composition of the presbyteral council and the college of consultors is reserved to priests. The finance committee, which is also mandatory, could be composed entirely of clerics if the bishop so desires. On the other hand, the only organizations which must include lay persons – the diocesan synod and the diocesan pastoral council – are not compulsory. This means that a bishop could, in practice, govern his diocese without ever having to consult the laity. Of course, this is not the spirit of the legislation. This absence of mandatory lay involvement, on its own, shows the limits currently placed on lay persons in their role as assistants to the bishop's power of governance. How long can this situation last?

Regardless of the observations we might make to support the Code's hesitancy regarding the laity, we must not be led to believe that there would automatically be significant changes if the Code were revised today. The 1997 Instruction on *The Cooperation of Non-ordained Faithful in the Sacred Ministry of Priests*, in its content, in the number of signing dicasteries, and with the *in forma specifica* papal approval, leaves no doubt as to the legislator's intention in the actual Code. He was not overcome by the rapid and considerable involvement of lay persons in diocesan pastoral activities, no more than he was at the time of the promulgation of the Code or in the period immediately thereafter. On the other hand, one cannot blame the legislator for believing that only a priest can replace a priest, that the actual situation can only be temporary, and that it cannot be officialised by a legislation that would normalize the exceptional or the temporary. In the meantime, though, can a bishop do anything to involve more directly in the government of his diocese those who assist him in his teaching and sanctifying offices?

Before answering this question, it would be necessary to review some doctrinal and canonical principles relating to the power of governance and its exercise.

III. THE POWER OF GOVERNANCE

A. The object of the power of governance

The conciliar documents, like the Code, refer to the threefold power of teaching, sanctifying and governing, as if each could operate independently, with its own and exclusive object. We are already quite familiar with the objects of the power of teaching and sanctifying; and we know very well that the former is oriented toward the latter. They are both, I might add, the summary of the Church's mission: "Go forth and preach to all nations, baptizing them..." As for the power of governance, all is not said when declaring that it is exercised in legislative, executive and judicial powers, and that it can be delegated under certain conditions. This concerns only its juridical nature. But we do not legislate simply for the sake of legislating, just as executive and judicial powers are not separated from the mission of teaching or sanctifying entrusted to the bishop in his pastoral office.

What is a bishop doing when, by virtue of his power of governance, he decides to establish a catechetical office or a marriage preparation programme? He is simply applying his power of governance to its proper end: the greater welfare of the Church's mission, summarized by the terms *teaching* and *sanctifying*.

If we were to give but a linear interpretation of the triple power, we might forget that the power of governance has no *raison d'être* or objective other than the remaining two powers. It is an instrumental power whose object is first and foremost pastoral since it is intended for teaching and sanctifying. Even in its judicial and penal dimensions, does the power of governance not concern the rights and obligations received at baptism whereby a physical person is constituted a person in the Church?

In introducing the organism known now as the presbyteral council, *Presbyterorum ordinis* no. 7 refers to the bishops' *munus docendi, sanctificandi* and **pascendi** instead of to the usual *regendi*. In the perspective of this presentation, there is no better way to speak about the power of governance. Lay persons involved full-time in pastoral activities are, in practice, associated with the bishop's power of teaching and sanctifying in virtue of their baptism and an appropriate mandate. Therefore, what prevents them from being somehow associated to the power of governance, assisting the bishop in his decisions regarding the exercise of the offices of teaching and sanctifying? We will return to this in a few moments.

B. The exercise of the power of governance

When we refer to the exercise of the power of governance, there is no question of challenging the conciliar definition of a diocese (*CD* no. 11), which was taken up in canon 369 of the Code. This canon states that the bishop is the pastor of the diocese "with the cooperation of the *presbyterium*", thus leaving untouched the basic necessity of having a presbyteral council. However, in order to assist him in the direct governance of his diocese, is there not some means whereby he could associate priests, deacons, lay persons, and religious, who are all mandated to participate on a full-time basis in the exercise of his pastoral office? Any such mechanism would have to be different from the pastoral council, even if its composition were similar.

In support of an affirmative response, we could invoke the ecclesiology of communion, co-responsibility or the emergence of new ministries, whether they are formally recognized or not. These three reasons could be sufficient to justify the involvement of lay persons in pastoral activities. But, on their own, they cannot justify juridically a bishop's decision to establish some type of organization that is not exclusively composed of priests to assist him in the governance of his diocese. The legal or juridical basis of his decision is clear: a bishop "has all the ordinary, proper and immediate power required for the exercise of his pastoral office" (canon 381, §1). Obviously, this power must be exercised according to the law. If the bishop has a doubt regarding the limits of the exercise of this power regarding the involvement of those who are not priests, he can always think of the diocesan synod. He will see how far the legislator himself goes with the issue of lay cooperation in the exercise of the bishop's power of governance. The synod is in fact the only diocesan institution assisting in the bishop's governance in its legislative dimension. The diocesan synod used to be comprised solely of priests, but it must now include lay persons, who even usually make up the vast majority of its members, although most of them are not involved full-time in pastoral structures. Who would have said that the diocesan synod would some day no longer be an exclusively presbyteral institution?

A bishop has a wide margin of creativity in the governance of his diocese. He must not curb this creativity by conceiving law as a limit imposed on the exercise of his power. Rather, law protects more from arbitrary power than from initiatives taken for the advancement of the mission. Furthermore, the law cannot anticipate all situations. Canon 516, §2 calls upon the bishop's creative mind when it stipulates that "where some communities cannot be established as parishes or quasi-parishes, the diocesan bishop is to provide for their spiritual care **in some other way.**" This "other way" could be, for example, the establishment of grassroots communities, the appointment of chaplains for certain groups in special circumstances, or episcopal vicars for certain linguistic groups, and so on.

If the bishop's power must be exercised according to law, it must also be exercised according to the awareness that he has of his office and, consequently, according to his notion of power. It goes without saying that the difference can be enormous in practice, depending on whether power is seen as an instrument of service, as a palliative measure compensating for an absence of authority, or as an instrument of domination.

A lot has been said and written about power. We even have different schools of thought on this subject. And everything has probably not yet been said. We were delighted when the second Vatican Council determined that the triple office of teaching, sanctifying and governing had a unique source in the laying of the hands. Yet, according to *Lumen gentium*'s *Nota explicativa praevia* (no. 2), these *munera* cannot "be ordered to action [without] a canonical or juridical determination through hierarchical authority." This changes very little in relation to the pre-Vatican II teaching on the dual origin of power (order and jurisdiction). Moreover, it is possible to exercise a true power (judicial power) without the laying on of hands. This is our present situation. Evidently, our acceptance of the consequences depends to some extent on to which school of thought a person subscribes.

Any remarks we might make on the subject of power, basing ourselves solely on the General Norms, would not be adequate when considering its exercise as outlined in the other Books of the Code. Book I, for instance, does not refer to the powers of teaching or sanctifying, but only the power of governing, the most juridical of the three. Then again, it refers to its function without mentioning the object of its application. Indeed, there is no reference to pastoral action nor to the source of power.

We must recognize, furthermore, that the object of the power of governance is disseminated throughout the Code. Book I refers to the nature of the power of governance; the other Books refer to its exercise. Canon 469 on the diocesan curia illustrates this point: "The diocesan curia is composed of those institutes and persons who assist the Bishop in governing the entire diocese, especially in directing pastoral action, in providing for the administration of the diocese, and in exercising judicial power."

Canon 469 is the only text in the Code where we can find a description, not of the power of governance, but of its content and its application to the government of the diocese. Nevertheless, this description is incomplete, as the use of the term "especially" (*praesertim*) suggests, implying that there might be more to governing than pastoral action, administration and the exercise of judicial power. But, in spite of the fact that canon 469 does not give a complete overview of possibilities, it does provide a new and insightful approach to the power of governance that could adequately support a bishop's decision to establish, for instance, a council of full-time pastoral ministers, including clerics and lay persons. Such a council, according to the mind of canon 469, would "assist [him] in governing the entire diocese, especially in directing pastoral action, administering the diocese, and exercising judicial power." This leads us to the principal point I wish to raise.

IV. A COUNCIL FOR ALL PASTORAL MINISTERS?

A. Nature and function of a pastoral ministers council

If a diocesan bishop were to establish a council for lay pastoral ministers, this council would, of course, be consultative in nature as are most of the bishop's councils. In no way would its establishment imply the elimination or replacement of the diocesan pastoral council or the presbyteral council.

i. Differences with the diocesan pastoral council

As with the diocesan pastoral council, the pastoral ministers council would be composed of priests, lay persons, religious, and permanent deacons. Although the members of the diocesan pastoral council must reflect the social conditions of the portion of the people of God which constitutes the diocese, the members of this new council would also represent the various ministers and ordained ministries, recognized or baptismal, working full-time in the diocese.

Naturally, the pastoral council could already have in its membership several lay persons involved full-time in pastoral work. This risks giving it an orientation which differs from its original purpose. If full-time ministers could be heard by the bishop through an organization representing them, the pastoral council could reassume its role of providing grassroots representation of the ministered people of God. It could inform the bishop of his people's needs and propose practical solutions. The bishop should, however, ensure that the number of permanent or full-time persons in ministry be limited within the pastoral council in order to encourage a broader sampling of the diocesan faithful to voice their opinion.

ii. *Differences with the presbyteral council*

Even if this proposed pastoral ministers council would assist the bishop in the governance of the diocese, it would not replace the presbyteral council whose necessary existence rests on the sacramental fraternity uniting a bishop and his priests. *Presbyterorum ordinis* refers to "communion in the same priesthood and the same ministry." It is however evident that the role of the presbyteral council would be somewhat modified if a new council were established. Since it represents the presbyterium who are the bishop's collaborators, it would continue advising him in matters prescribed by law. It is also the body from which certain members are chosen to constitute the college of consultors. The bishop could continue seeking its advice on pastoral or administrative matters. As it would be relieved of part of its responsibilities, the presbyteral council would have to avoid the temptation of concentrating itself merely on questions concerning the welfare of priests. This pertains either to the bishop (canon 384) or to a personnel office. As several of its customary functions would be transferred to the pastoral ministers council, the number of its members could be reduced. There can be no less than six, however, which is the minimum number of members for the college of consultors. Could the presbyteral council fulfill the responsibilities of the college of consultors if the number of its members is between six and twelve? The law does not forbid nor permit it. It seems to me, though, that this is not the spirit of the law.

In most dioceses, the presbyteral council meets occasionally to advise the bishop on matters defined by law, for the sake of the validity of the decision. More often, the presbyteral council meets to reflect on diocesan orientations and policies, as well as on questions submitted by the bishop or proposed by the council. In general, as suggested in canon 500, §2, the bishop consults it "in matters of more serious moment." The council frequently creates a study committee to prepare the files which the council will later consider. Henceforth these duties could be assigned to the pastoral ministers council, without prejudice to questions the bishop might wish to continue submitting to the presbyteral council. These same questions could have been just as easily studied beforehand by the pastoral ministers council and the pastoral council. Of course, the opposite is equally true.

B. The role of the proposed new council

This new council, if it were established, would constitute an ideal environment for recognizing the complementarity of ministries. It would also provide a privileged setting for information regarding the needs of the faithful, developing responses to these needs, and seeking to overcome the difficulties in meeting them. It would also be an ideal arena for exchanging creative ideas in implementing these services. Finally, as is the case with the presbyteral council (canon 501, §2), when the see is vacant, the new council would lapse.

The pastoral ministers council would not be a council of the lay apostolate. Rather, it would bring together ordained ministers, religious, and lay persons, mandated by the bishop to participate full-time in the exercise of his pastoral office. Presided over by the bishop, and somewhat modelled on the presbyteral council, it would comprise *ex officio* members, as well as representatives of other categories of pastoral ministers, permanent deacons, priests, and religious. It could also reflect the pastoral regions of the diocese. Finally, the bishop could freely appoint a few members to ensure adequate representation. Among the *ex officio* members of the bishop's various councils, the judicial vicar is very often forgotten. Experience shows, however, that in the Church it is possible to act unfairly out of kindness. The opposite is also true. It would be desirable that an organization such as the pastoral ministers council include a member in charge of ensuring justice and equity. Let us not forget that conflict situations involving both canonical and civil laws seem to be multiplying in certain sectors or cultures.

CONCLUSION

Where does this leave us? The establishment of a council of pastoral ministers seems to be, in my perspective, a legitimate application of canon 129, §2: "Lay members of Christ's faithful can cooperate in the exercise of [the power of governance] in accordance with the law." The text does not specify which law. It could therefore be in accordance with particular law.

Moreover, without seeming to consecrate a situation which must be seen as temporary, that is the shortage of priests, it is evident that the bishop will not be able to overlook indefinitely the point of view of the lay persons he mandates to work full-time in the Church's mission.

These persons are often the only ones occupying certain pastoral positions formerly reserved to priests. They frequently witness difficulties and needs in a diocese which the bishop risks not being able to overcome or fulfill adequately if he does not have the advantage of their indispensable point of view.

It is quite evident that the establishment of such an organization would not be without question. We have tried to answer some of these concerns regarding its theological basis and its juridical legitimacy. The fact remains that the bishop would find himself with one more council, as if he didn't have enough already! And, then, at least at the beginning, this council's field of competency would not always be easy to determine in relation to pastoral and presbyteral councils. At the same time, it would be very important to ensure the *ex officio* presence of certain persons in each of these councils, such as the moderator of the curia, or the coordinator of pastoral activities, or, if need be, the vicar general. Moreover, each council would be presided over by the bishop who retains his freedom concerning the issues to be considered, given that he is not a member of any council. Finally, practical experience will show how this proposed new council could become relevant.

The diocesan pastoral council would have a somewhat reduced number of full-time lay ministers in its membership. Could this allow it to rediscover its true *raison d'être*? It could appear that the presbyteral council has the most to lose with this initiative. That is not totally false, since an important part of its role would be passed on to the new council; its meetings would necessarily be less frequent, and the number of members would be reduced. Additionally, even the matters about which it must advise the bishop in virtue of the law, such as the establishment or suppression of parishes, would probably also be discussed with the new council. No longer would the gratifying feeling of belonging to a select group of counsellors to the bishop be the motivation for accepting a mandate on the presbyteral council.

The fact remains, however, that the presbyterium would still be represented in the new council and that it would be enriched by the sharing of experiences of other ministers working in areas where priests can no longer be as present as they were before because of their now diminished numbers.

KERKELIJKE RECHTBANKEN *SECUNDUM* EN *PRAETER LEGEM*

Rik Torfs

De gloriedagen van de *societas perfecta* zijn voorbij[1]. Vrijwel niemand haalt het dus nog in zijn hoofd om de kerk als dusdanig te omschrijven. Betekent dit dan dat we vandaag uitsluitend te maken hebben met de kerk als *communio*, als Volk Gods of als Lichaam van Christus? Op het vlak van de officiële toespraken en de theologische bespiegelingen lijkt het vaak zo. Maar, en ik vertel hier niets nieuws, het *societas perfecta*-denken is niet dood[2]. Omdat structuren sterker zijn dan ideeën? Misschien. Maar niet uitsluitend. Want soms geldt het omgekeerde, en zijn ideeën sterker dan structuren, zoals de politieke vertaling van de Verlichtingsideeën in een aantal landen heeft bewezen.

Er is nog een andere reden waarom de schaduw van de *societas perfecta* over het kerkelijk recht blijft hangen, namelijk deze: er is geen onmiddellijk zichtbaar alternatief. Allemaal goed en wel, een kerk als *communio*, maar hoe zit die canoniek dan wel in elkaar? Het moet toch om meer gaan dan de juridische uittekening van de *afwezigheid* van het oude model? Of bestaat er zoiets als 'negatief kerkelijk recht'? Die vragen zijn ongemeen boeiend. Te boeiend misschien voor een canonist. Daarom stel ik ze niet. Ik zou eerder willen beginnen met een eenvoudige beschrijving, niet van mogelijke nieuwe normen *de lege ferenda*, maar van de moeizame exodus uit de *societas perfecta*-gedachte. Hoe maakt de mens zich los van iets waarvan hij niet houdt, maar dat hij toch niet kan missen? Die vraag behandel ik eerst, met alle consequenties die aan het probleem verbonden zijn, dus met inbegrip van gemiste kansen en onvermoede problemen. Vanuit een beschrijving van het bestaande denkklimaat land ik dan bij de kerkelijke rechtbank aan. Kan zij in het huidige tijdsgewricht binnenkerkelijk een rol van betekenis spelen? Een andere dan vandaag? En, zo ja, welke dan, en hoe?

---

[1] P. GRANFIELD, "Het verschijnen en verdwijnen van de societas perfecta", *Concilium* 1982, n° 7, 8-14.

[2] R. TORFS, "The Roman Catholic Church and Secular Legal Culture in the Twentieth Century", *Studia Historiae Ecclesiasticae* 1999, 1-20.

EXODUS UIT HET *SOCIETAS PERFECTA*-DENKEN

Wat doen bisschoppen, kerkjuristen, bestuurders die altijd al stilzwijgend in een *societas perfecta* werkzaam zijn geweest en plots te horen krijgen dat de onderliggende theologische vooronderstellingen niet helemaal kloppen? In het slechtste geval wachten zij hun opruststelling af. Maar doorgaans zullen zij een uitweg zoeken die nieuwe ideeën integreert zonder dat hun *modus vivendi* compleet moet veranderen. Heel concreet heeft dit, binnenkerkelijk, tot een werkwijze in twee gradaties geleid.

Een eerste mogelijke reactie op de neergang van de *societas perfecta*-gedachte bestaat erin *ratione materiae* in te binden. Eigenlijk betekent dit dat de kerkelijke overheid even autonoom denkt en zich even onafhankelijk gedraagt als voorheen. Maar het *terrein* waarop dit zelfstandige bestaan zich afspeelt is kleiner dan voorheen, sluit nauwer aan bij het religieuze en spirituele in strikte zin. Kortom, de kerk blijft net zo autonoom als voorheen, maar het speelveld is beperkter. Die aanpak kan op verschillende wijzen in de praktijk worden gebracht. Bijvoorbeeld door meer in te zoomen op kerkrechtelijke materies die specifiek religieus zijn, zoals sacramentenrecht of liturgisch recht. De indruk bestaat dat meer topcanonisten dan vroeger precies in die sectoren actief te zijn. Terecht uiteraard, en met veel succes, ik denk hier aan auteurs zoals John Huels[3]. Maar tegelijk is het zo dat wie in dit soort materies opereert, wellicht het verwijt niet treft dat hij met het juridische ordenen van een parallelle samenleving bezig is. Hier komen we soms uit bij wat men een *ius perfectum* zou kunnen noemen[4]. De kerk is misschien geen volmaakte maatschappij die op zichzelf staat. Maar het recht dat zij uitvaardigt en hanteert, heeft een volkomen andere dynamiek dan het profane. Het is vriendelijker, zachter, pastoraler, corrigeert op tijd en stond zijn eigen hardheid. Daarbij valt het volgende op: ofschoon het *ius perfectum* in feite een autonoom werkveld creëert op een manier die niet eens zoveel van de *societas perfecta* verschilt, is het discours bescheidener. Het kerkelijk recht ontpopt zich niet langer tot een rivaal van het profane. Rivaliteit is trouwens een lelijk woord. Canoniek recht staat voor zachte waarden. Het is zacht als zijde. Zo ongeveer luidt, impliciet, de onderliggende gedachte. De werkelijkheid is natuurlijk complexer. Het is bijvoorbeeld niet omdat sacramenten een solide theologische basis hebben, dat een harde juridische omgang ermee uitgesloten is.

---

[3] Zie bijvoorbeeld J.M. HUELS, *More Disputed Questions in Liturgy*, Chicago, Liturgy Training Publications, 1996, vi + 200 p.; J.M. HUELS, "Principles of Liturgical Adaptation in Light of Justice and Forgiveness", *CLSA Proceedings* 1999, 1-25.

[4] R. TORFS, *l.c.*, 13-14.

Schijnbare bescheidenheid dook ook op in de canonieke discussie in
de periode tussen concilie en codex toen licht exotische experimenten
schering en inslag waren. De term *strafrecht* lag toen minder goed in de
markt, *tuchtrecht* leek bescheidener. Op die manier werd nog eens impliciet afstand genomen van een *societas perfecta*-context. Tuchtrecht
is immers het recht van een bepaalde deelgroep, zoals een beroepsver-
eniging of een sportbond, binnen een ruimere en algemeen erkende
maatschappelijke context. De *societas perfecta* wordt verlaten door het
werkveld van de kerkelijke autonomie in te perken. Binnen dat werkveld hanteert de kerk een geheel eigen recht, een soort van *ius perfectum*. Een enkele keer sloeg dat *ius perfectum* zelfs aan bij profane juristen. Dat was zo voor de straffen *latae sententiae*. Daarmee was iets heel
vreemds aan de hand. In het negende van de tien beginselen die de algemene vergadering van de bisschoppensynode in 1967 goedkeurde als
belangrijkste principes die aan het nieuwe kerkelijke wetboek ten
grondslag moesten liggen[5], werd op een maximaal elimineren van *latae
sententiae*-straffen aangedrongen. Tegelijk vonden progressieve profane juristen die rechtsfiguur net verfrissend: de delinquent werd
immers echt ernstig genomen. Hij werd met de analyse en beoordeling
van zijn eigen misdrijf belast. Even ontstond er een vreemd verbond
tussen de *latae sententiae*-straffen en de permissieve samenleving.
Even maar natuurlijk: meestal kwam het *ius perfectum* niet voor export
in aanmerking.

De tweede mogelijke canonieke reactie gaat een stap verder. De kerkelijke overheid plooit zich niet uitsluitend terug op vertrouwd religieus
terrein. Het kerkelijk wetboek, de legislatieve activiteiten van de wetgever, de actieradius van de kerkjurist krimpen niet meteen in. Alleen wordt
aan kerkrechtelijke activiteiten, ook als ze er erg profaan uitzien, een
andere kwalificatie en een andere naam gegeven. Zenon Grocholewski[6]

---

[5] "Principia quae codicis iuris canonici recognitionem dirigant", *Communicationes*
1969, 84-85:
"DE RECOGNOSCENDO IURE POENALI
9. In recognitione iuris poenalis Ecclesiae, principium reducendi poenas in Codice stabilitas, nemo est qui non accepet. Verum suppressionem omnium poenarum ecclesiasticarum, cum ius coactivum, cuiuslibet societatis perfectae proprium, ab Ecclesia abiudicari
nequeat, nemo canonistarum admittere videtur.
Mens est ut poenae generatim sint ferendae sententiae et in solo foro externo irrogentur et remittantur. Quod ad poenas latae sententiae attinet, etsi a non paucis earum abolitio proposita sit, mens est ut illae ad paucos omnino casus reducantur, imo ad paucissima
eaque gravissima delicta."
[6] Z. GROCHOLEWSKI, "De ordinatione ac munere tribunalium in ecclesia ratione quoque habita iustitiae administrativae", *Ephemerides Iuris Canonici* 1992, 75.

bijvoorbeeld onderlijnt dat zogenaamd "administratieve" conflicten ook een spirituele dimensie hebben[7].

Kernschetsend in dit verband is een verhaal dat de Duitse canonist Norbert Ruf enkele jaren geleden vertelde[8]. Voor het *Landgericht* van Freiburg werd een aartspriester van de Russisch-geünieerde kerk wegens zedenfeiten aangeklaagd. Maar daarvoor had er reeds een canoniek strafproces plaatsgevonden voor de kerkelijke rechtbank van Freiburg, en zulks in opdracht van de Congregatie voor de Geloofsleer. De advocaat van de aartspriester vroeg aan de profane rechtbank om de officiaal als getuige op te roepen. Maar deze laatste beriep zich op zijn hoedanigheid van zielzorger, waardoor hij volgens het Duitse recht niet moest getuigen. Een officiaal als zielzorger? Hoe zo dan, vroeg de profane rechter zich af. De officiaal antwoordde in het Latijn: *salus animarum in Ecclesia suprema semper lex esse debet*, naar de slotzin van canon 1752. De profane rechtbank, en later de beroepsinstantie, namen vrede met deze uitleg. De aartspriester, van zijn kant, werd tot twee jaar gevangenisstraf veroordeeld. Natuurlijk niet *omdat* de officiaal een zielzorger was, hoewel hij precies daarom niet hoefde te getuigen.

Maar niet alleen de officiaal treedt als zielzorger op, ook de gewone kerkelijke rechter, zoals Karl-Heinz Selge heeft beschreven[9]. Selge onderscheidt *cura animarum* van *cura pastoralis*, waarbij laatstgenoemde ruimer is en zielzorg impliceert. Uit de bekende canon 517 §2 die over pastorale zorg over een parochie bij priestertekort handelt, blijkt trouwens dat ook leken pastorale zorg kunnen uitoefenen, dus *a fortiori* zielzorg. Selge verantwoordt trouwens mooi waarom het ambt van kerkelijk rechter een ambt in de zielzorg is. Zijn redenering gaat als volgt: voor zover de rechter via zijn jurisprudentie de directe lokale zielzorg helpt te verwerkelijken, oefent hij *middellijke* zielzorg uit. Ofschoon het bij die rechtspraak ook om een pastorale dienst gaat, heeft de rechter niet automatisch met zielzorg in de strikte zin te maken. Hij treedt echter wel

[7] Zie ook de studie van A.J.T. VAN DEN HOUT, *L'ecclesialità del processo contenzioso-ordinario e del contenzioso-amministrativo*, Rome, Pontificium Athenaeum Sanctae Crucis, 1998, 330 p.

[8] N. RUF, "Zum pastoralen Standort des Diözesangerichtes", in R. PUZA en A. WEIß (ed.), *Iustitia in caritate. Festgabe für Ernst Rößler zum 25jährigen Dienstjubiläum als Offizial der Diözese Rottenburg-Stuttgart*, in E. GÜTHOFF en K.-H. SELGE (ed.), *Adnotationes in ius canonicum*, III, Frankfurt am Main/Berlijn/Bern/New York/Parijs/Wenen, Peter Lang, 1997, 396-405.

[9] K.-H. SELGE, "Der kirchliche Richter als Seelsorger im ordentlichen Ehenichtigkeitsverfahren erster Instanz", in E. GÜTHOFF en K.-H. SELGE (ed.), *Festgabe F.X. Walter zur Vollendung des 65. Lebensjahres*, Fredersdorf, Rodak, 1994, 31.

als zielzorger op indien hij tijdens de procedure taken waarneemt, die met de individuele zielzorg te maken hebben. Zijn zielzorg is hier *onmiddellijk*, ofschoon zijn rechtersambt maar ten dele met zielzorg verbonden is. Hoofdopgave blijft immers het organiseren van een vakbekwame procesvoering. Zijn ambt is derhalve geen monofunctioneel, maar een multifunctioneel ambt in de zielzorg. Die facetten komen onder meer naar boven wanneer de rechter persoonlijke raad geeft of concrete toelichtingen bij het proces verschaft[10].

Het verhaal van Ruf en de mooi opgebouwde redenering van Selge tonen aan hoe zelfs in het procesrecht - een niet meteen bevlogen rechtstak die heel wat technische vaardigheden vereist - een louter juridische benadering in vraag wordt gesteld. De man die oordeelt is een pastor.

Duidelijk wordt hoe een andere benadering van recht, een soort van *ius perfectum*-denken, het canonieke recht in toenemende mate kleurt. De nieuwe, schijnbaar zachtere, rechtsvisie, blijft niet beperkt tot typisch kerkelijke sectoren zoals het liturgisch recht, de leertaak of het sacramentenrecht. Ze transformeert ook de administratieve procedure en maakt de rechter tot zielzorger. Kortom, het hele terrein van de oude *societas perfecta* wordt langzaam door het *ius perfectum* veroverd[11].

Achter het officiële beeld schuilen spanningsvelden. Niet alleen bestaat er een zekere tensie tussen zielzorg en het oordelen als rechter, zeker in concreto. Bovendien zijn de zoektocht naar de waarheid en procesrechtelijke strakheid niet altijd moeiteloos combineerbaar. Toch niet in de praktijk. Formalisme dat op het vlak van procedures nooit compleet te vermijden is, bedreigt misschien de zielzorg, maar in zekere zin ook de waarheid[12]. Een procedurefout die tot de nietigheid van een oordeel[13] leidt dat materieelrechtelijk onomstotelijk met de waarheid

---

[10] K.-H. SELGE, *l.c.*, 41.

[11] Een ander voorbeeld. Plichten en rechten van alle christengelovigen lijken dicht bij de mensenrechten in de profane samenleving te staan. Maar dat is alleen maar schijn. Theologische en ecclesiologische ideeën maken dat het verschil wezenlijk is. Zie J. HERRANZ CASADO, "Renewal and Effectiveness in Canon Law", *Studia Canonica* 1994, 5-31.

[12] Gelijkaardige spanningen zijn zichtbaar bij de discussie over de vraag of het procesrecht nu het subjectieve recht dan wel het objectieve recht verdedigt. Zie F. ROBERTI, *De processibus*, Rome, Pontificium Institutum Utriusque Iuris, 1941, p. 73-74, nr. 26: "Omnes moderni doctores finem processus iuris actuationem statuunt; inter se autem non conveniunt cum agitur de statuendo proprio eius fine. Etenim plures affirmant processum formaliter ordinari ad exsecutionem iuris obiectivi seu legis, indirecte vero tueri iura subiectiva. Alii contra contendunt finem proximum esse exsecutionem iuris subiectivi, ex qua indirecte etiam ius obiectivum exsecutioni mandatur."

[13] Zie, over bepaalde facetten hiervan, M. THÉRIAULT, "The Nullity of Some Processual Acts in Light of Canon 124", *Forum* 1994, nr. 1, 29-42.

strookt, is daar een interessante illustratie van. Procesrecht is vaak te hard voor wie pastor is, en te bochtig voor wie de waarheid zoekt[14].

Maar even terug nu naar de exodus uit de wereld van de *societas perfecta*. Die wordt niet zozeer gekenmerkt door de impliciete vraag naar structuren die aan theologische vernieuwingen beantwoorden. Wat eerder speelt is: hoe blijft een traditionele, sterk autonome, manier van werken overeind zonder dat de kerk als *societas perfecta* als onderliggende basis kan blijven fungeren. De uitweg bestond in eerste instantie uit een *ratione materiae*-terugtocht op vertrouwd theologisch gekleurd terrein en dat geschiedde via een *ius perfectum*. In een tweede fase beïnvloedt de theologisch gekleurde *ius perfectum*-aanpak het gehele recht.

De geschetste werkwijze, zowel in haar eerste, schuchtere, versie als in haar tweede wat meer gedurfde gedaante, is manifest defensief. De canonist plooit zich terug. Omdat hij de schijn niet meer hoog wil houden met de juridische omkadering van de *societas perfecta* bezig te zijn, wordt hij dan maar een uitermate theologisch geïnspireerd canonist, een zielzorger zelfs. Dat heeft gevolgen. In een maatschappelijke context waarin het recht gewoonweg alomtegenwoordig is, wordt de canonist op juridisch vlak een amateur. Hij fungeert binnen helder getrokken krijtlijnen en volgt de eigen logica van het canonieke recht. Botst de benadering van de canonist met het profane recht, dan moeten veelal dure profane juristen worden ingehuurd om te redden wat er te redden valt. Zij kunnen er bijvoorbeeld op wijzen dat een goed begrepen godsdienstvrijheid ook een behoorlijke brok autonomie voor kerken vereist. Vele bisschoppen hechten trouwens meer belang aan de visie van de profane advocaat die hen *ad extra* verdedigt, dan aan de opinie van de canonist die nooit een gevaarlijk tegenspeler is. In een specifiek kerkelijke context kan hij altijd volkomen legaal worden geneutraliseerd.

Met die aanpak heb ik het erg moeilijk, en dat dan vooral omwille van twee redenen die ongetwijfeld theologisch kunnen worden vertaald, maar die in wezen niet tot de theologie behoren.

De eerste reden is de treurnis en uitzichtloosheid die met een defensieve strategie gepaard gaat. Wie zijn grenzen, zijn bezit, zijn rechtspositie alleen maar verdedigt, bouwt niet op. Bovendien groeit, merkwaardig genoeg, na een tijdje de indruk dat wat verdedigd wordt, niet iets heel rechtmatigs is, maar een privilege. Een indruk zoals die bij de ver-

---

[14] Een contradictie tussen *iustitia* en *veritas* bestaat op het theoretische vlak natuurlijk allerminst. Zie over dit onderwerp Z. GROCHOLEWSKI, "Iustitia ecclesiastica et veritas", *Periodica* 1995, 7-30.

dediging van Fort Europa ook soms bestaat. Er komt argwaan. Wie absoluut iets wil behouden, meent wellicht dat hij er in de toekomst niet in zal slagen om op legitieme wijze iets gelijkaardigs te verwerven. Wat er nu is, komt nooit terug als het ooit zou verdwijnen.

Maar er is meer. Gezien de rijke traditie van de canonistiek, de invloed ook die ze op het profane recht uitoefende, is het beschamend te moeten vaststellen dat zijzelf nu om theologische redenen voor een benadering van recht zou kiezen die algemeen maatschappelijk niet echt relevant meer is. Als een theologische benadering van canoniek recht betekent dat het voortaan geen echt recht meer is, maar een formele legitimatie van het heersende theologische denken, dan is de prijs toch wel erg hoog. Moet en kan aan deze defensieve houding en juridisch-technische abdicatie iets worden gedaan? Dat wordt dan toch wel de vraag.

Ik denk dat het inderdaad kan en moet. Wat immers door kerkleiders wordt onderschat, is de onheilspellende gedachte dat een strategische terugtocht *ratione materiae* of op methodologisch vlak, nog niet betekent dat de profane rechter zich van interventies in binnenkerkelijke aangelegenheden zal blijven onthouden. Monseigneur Ruud Huysmans had het hierover naar aanleiding van de tweejaarlijkse studiebijeenkomst van de Werkgroep Nederlandstalige Canonisten (WNC) in december 2000: het eigen kerkrecht speelt nauwelijks bij problemen die de profane samenleving aanbelangen, zoals burgerlijke aansprakelijkheid bij seksueel misbruik[15]. Natuurlijk verbaast zoiets op het eerst gezicht: de kerk bestrijkt minder terrein, of doet het anders, dan toen ze zich nog als *societas perfecta* profileerde, ze lijkt dus minder ambitieus, en toch krijgt ze vaker dan voorheen met interventies van de profane rechter te maken. Dat kan uiteraard allen maar als de strategische terugtocht van de kerk gepaard gaat met een alsmaar expansiever profane recht, een profaan recht dat meer terrein bezet en dwingender wordt in zijn regelgeving.

AANSLUITING BIJ DE MODERNE SAMENLEVING

De voortschrijdende juridisering van de moderne samenleving is voor sommigen een spijtige illustratie van een allesoverheersend individualisme. Altijd maar rechten en nooit plichten. De klaagzang is bekend. Maar ofschoon excessen niet afwezig blijven, mag ook het emancipa-

---

[15] R.G.W. HUYSMANS, "Geen rol kerkrecht in kwestie aansprakelijkheid bisschop", *1 2 1* 2000, 695-696.

toire aspect van het recht niet worden vergeten. Mensenrechten brachten bijvoorbeeld na de tweede wereldoorlog echte bevrijding mee, die ten tijde van het nationaal-socialisme ver te zoeken was. Kortom, ondanks het risico van overdrijvingen, kan een goed uitgebouwd kerkelijk recht een gewaardeerd contactpunt vormen tussen kerk en wereld. Binnen deze voortrekkersfunctie voor het recht in het algemeen, lijkt vooral de rol van de rechtbanken en hun jurisprudentie van groot belang. Met enige zin voor overdrijving kan de gedachte worden geformuleerd dat de toekomst van het kerkelijk recht afhangt van het al dan niet functioneren van de tribunalen. Als een norm op dat echelon niet kan worden geanalyseerd en geïnterpreteerd, blijft hij een loutere programmaverklaring, profileert hij zich voornamelijk ideologisch ten koste van zijn juridische slagkracht.

Een probleem is nu dat er met de kerkelijke rechtbank een en ander schort. Daarmee bedoel ik allerminst dat de meeste kerkelijke rechtbanken niet goed zouden functioneren. Het tegendeel is waar. Maar ze kampen wel met een dubbele handicap. Ze fungeren in een systeem waarin geen scheiding of evenwicht van machten bestaat. En ze houden zich vrijwel uitsluitend met huwelijkszaken bezig. Die dubbele handicap is trouwens wellicht minder dubbel dan hij lijkt: juist *omdat* scheiding van machten in de kerk niet wordt aanvaard, blijft de rechtbank niet veel anders over dan zich op het pastoraal erg ingrijpende, maar kerkpolitiek redelijk onbelangrijke huwelijksrecht te storten. Op andere terreinen valt niet veel te bereiken. Rechtbanken zijn immers onvoldoende onafhankelijk.

Kan het anders? Ik laat even alle *de lege ferendae* oplossingen buiten beschouwing. Ook kwaliteitsvereisten voor het canonieke proces, zoals Salvatore Berlingò die reeds in 1993 formuleerde, laat ik achterwege[16]. Berlingò vermeldde drie eisen, waarvan de publicatie van de akten voor de partijen en het reële technische recht op verdediging ook vandaag haalbaar zijn. Zijn derde punt, het duidelijke onderscheid tussen de partijen en het beslissingsorgaan alsmede de onafhankelijkheid van de rechter, ligt al gevoeliger. Om het echt te concretiseren moet er een vorm van scheiding van machten komen. Maar de afwezigheid daarvan heeft in de ogen van velen een theologische basis. De droom van een onafhankelijke kerkelijke rechtbank mag dus niet voor een spoedig te realiseren werkelijkheid worden genomen.

---

[16] S. BERLINGÒ, "Il diritto al 'processo' (can. 221 § 2 CIC) in alcune procedure particolari", *Persona y Derecho. Suplemento 'Fidelium iura' de derecho y deberes fundamentales del fiel* 1993, 339-358, i.c. 354-357.

Wèl kerkrechtelijk aanvaardbaar en met wat goede wil haalbaar is een particulierrechtelijke constructie, waarbij de kerkelijke rechtbank wordt opgenomen in een meer omvattende juridische dienst[17]. Natuurlijk dient canon 135 §3 altijd in het vizier te blijven: rechterlijke macht, die rechters of rechterlijke colleges bezitten, moet worden uitgeoefend op de wijze door het recht voorgeschreven, en kan niet worden gedelegeerd, tenzij voor het stellen van handelingen die een decreet of een vonnis voorbereiden. Problemen op dat terrein kunnen mijns inziens worden voorkomen door de juridische dienst ruimer op te vatten dan exclusief als een orgaan van de rechterlijke macht[18]. Die rechterlijke macht speelt in het voorstel een dubbele rol, is een scharnier. Ze blijft deel uitmaken van de drie machten die in canon 135 §1 worden opgesomd[19]. En tegelijk vormt zij een centraal gedeelte van de op te richten juridische dienst. Wat dus de wetgevende, uitvoerende en rechterlijke macht aangaat, blijft het plaatje wat het was.

De rechtspraak vertegenwoordigt één van de drie machten, maar *de iure* ontbreken administratieve rechtbanken op diocesaan vlak en *de facto* blijken ook gewone contentieuze processen nauwelijks voor te komen. Maximaal is er sprake - en hier verschilt de situatie van land tot land - van een *revival* van het strafproces. Daarom ook dat bij een grafische voorstelling van de binnenkerkelijke *trias politica* de rechtspraak een beperkter terrein bestrijkt dan de wetgeving en de uitvoerende macht.

Maar welke diensten buiten de traditionele rechtbank zouden door een toekomstige juridische dienst dan moeten worden aangeboden? Alvast

---

[17] De juridische dienst heeft te maken met het toepassingsgebied en de speelruimte van het kerkelijk recht. Uiteraard blijven ook andere punten belangrijk, zoals een verbeterde werking, rationele organisatie en kritische zelfevaluatie van de kerkelijke rechtbank. Zie daarover onder andere M.A. HACK, "Selected Issues in the Administration of a Diocesan Tribunal (Everything They Don't Teach in Canon Law Class)", *CLSA Proceedings* 1996, 187-209.

[18] Een ruimere opvatting kan natuurlijk ook binnen de rechterlijke macht, onder meer door particulierrechtelijke uitbreiding van de bestaande mogelijkheden of door een betere aanwending van wat nu al bestaat. Zie over deze en andere zaken het erg creatieve artikel van K. LÜDICKE, "Möglichkeit und Notwendigkeit einer partikularrechtlichen kirchlichen Gerichtsbarkeit in Deutschland", *De Processibus Matrimonialibus* 1999, 55-70.

[19] E. CORECCO, "Nature et structure de la *sacra potestas* dans la doctrine et dans le nouveau code de droit canonique", *Revue de droit canonique* 1984, 389 ziet het loutere feit van deze indeling in drie machten een betreurenswaardige theologische regressie.

zou hij bestaande particuliere procedures moeten bundelen, of ze nu con-
flictvermijdend zijn zoals diocesane verzoeningsbureaus in het raam van
canon 1733 opgericht, of bijzondere procedures instellen zoals bijvoorbeeld betreffende seksueel misbruik of de vrijheid van meningsuiting
van de theoloog. Zijn die gremia onafhankelijk of maken ze deel uit van
rechterlijke colleges in de zin van canon 135 §3? Dat hangt volkomen af
van hoe de desbetreffende particuliere normen zijn opgesteld, al kan de
bisschop enerzijds wel aan zelfbinding doen, maar anderzijds de rechten
die hem volgens canon 381 toekomen niet definitief vervreemden.

Een laatste luik van de juridische dienst valt in het preventieve werk
te situeren. Het opstellen van algemene statuten of concrete contracten
die conflicten op een afstand houden, hoort daar beslist bij. Uiteraard
komen ook snijvlakken met het profane recht aan de orde, zodat de formele inschakeling of structurele medewerking van seculiere juristen hier
noodzakelijk is. Dat alles leidt tot het volgende plaatje.

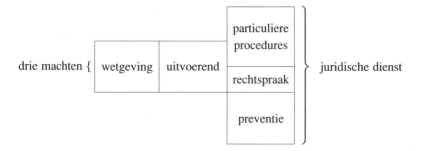

Opvallend is dat de traditionele rechterlijke macht het scharnierpunt is
waar de horizontale as (de drie machten) en de verticale (de juridische
dienst) elkaar ontmoeten. De juridische dienst corrigeert ook de onvol-
maaktheid van de horizontale as, door de qua reikwijdte beperkte rechterlijke macht verder uit te bouwen. Wat de traditionele rechterlijke
macht aan procedures *niet* biedt, kan door de particuliere procedures
worden opgevangen. En tegelijk kunnen particuliere procedures in het
leven worden geroepen die niet tot de rechterlijke macht behoren.
Externe arbitrage hoort hier mijns inziens thuis.

De voorgestelde constructie ziet er betrekkelijk voor de hand liggend
uit, maar grijpt dieper in het systeem in dan een oppervlakkig waarne-
mer zou vermoeden. De juridische dienst brengt immers het profane
recht weer dichter bij het canonieke. De rechterlijke macht komt ver-
zwakt uit de louter kerkelijke benadering te voorschijn: omdat er geen
evenwicht van machten is, bestrijkt de rechtspraak maar een fractie van

het terrein dat door de wetgeving en het bestuur wordt waargenomen. De aanvulling die er komt, situeert zich *praeter legem*. De bijzondere procedures waar het daarbij om gaat, zijn minder typisch kerkelijk dan de universele normen. Zij krijgen gestalte op lokaal niveau, de invloed en impliciete eisen van de profane rechtscultuur zullen nooit veraf zijn. Ook de eenheid van machten is wellicht aan amendering onderhevig. In een particuliere procedure die naar algemeen maatschappelijke geloofwaardigheid hengelt, is het onmogelijk de nadruk te leggen op de bisschop als opperste rechter. Zelfs deze gedachte vermelden, is contraproductief. Zo een aanpak stemt wellicht argwanend, terwijl de universeelrechtelijk bepaalde rol van de bisschop ook overeind blijft wanneer een particuliere procedure daar niet expliciet melding van maakt.

Anders uitgedrukt: een particuliere procedure onttrekt zich *de iure* niet aan het principe van eenheid van machten zoals bijvoorbeeld in canon 381 indirect uitgedrukt[20]. *De facto* blijkt dat beginsel evenwel psychologisch onhaalbaar te zijn. Onhaalbaar, en wellicht niet de bedoeling. Een bisschop die een particuliere procedure in het leven roept, is daartoe niet verplicht. De keuze voor het invoeren van zo een procedure, impliceert vanwege de bisschop een zekere wil tot machtsspreiding. Die wil kan structureel niet volledig worden gehonoreerd: als hij zich in een later stadium niet bij de uitkomst van door hemzelf ingevoerde 'machtsdelende' procedures wil neerleggen, kan hij daartoe wellicht niet worden gedwongen. Maar dan bevinden wij ons reeds op het terrein van de uitvoering. Bij de elaboratie van de particuliere procedure kan een ultieme wil tot voorbehoud nooit de boventoon voeren.

Bij *preventieve* activiteiten van de juridische dienst is de toenadering tot de wereld van het profane recht nog groter. Het preventieve werk slaat natuurlijk aan de ene kant op het vermijden van binnenkerkelijke conflicten. Aan de andere kant is het ook zaak spanningsvelden met de profane maatschappij tot een minimum te beperken. Preventief werk op dit terrein houdt tegelijk onderzoek in naar mogelijke profaanjuridische gevolgen van het beleid van de bisschop en zijn beleidsorganen. Tot slaafse navolging van maatschappelijke modetrends hoeft zoiets niet te leiden. Wèl is het nuttig dat eventuele profane rechtsgevolgen van het kerkelijke beleid vooraf kunnen worden gewikt en gewogen. Enkele mogelijke vragen: grijpt de profane rechter in als de bisschop beslissingen neemt zonder de voorgeschreven binnenkerkelijke procedure te volgen? Is de bisschop burgerrechtelijk aanspra-

---

[20] *Potestas* in canon 381 § 1 wordt immers als *potestas regiminis* gezien. Zie G. BIER, in *Münsterischer Kommentar zum CIC*, Essen, Ludgerus, sinds 1985 (losbladig; stand: 33.Erg.Lfg.Juni 2000), 381, 6.

kelijk voor de handelingen van zijn priesters? Voor *alle* handelingen? Van
al zijn priesters? Wanneer het antwoord op sommige van die vragen wat
onrustwekkend zou klinken, dan is het aan de bisschop om uit te maken wat
een eventueel 'profetisch' optreden hem zal kosten. Dat is dan het hoofd-
stuk kerkelijk recht en economie. In ieder geval, gezien de preventieve taak
beperkt blijft tot het verstrekken van adviezen, wordt ze normaal gezien niet
gehypothekeerd door het principe van eenheid van machten. Het kan zijn
dat de verstrekkers van preventie uit *metus reverentialis* er niet in slagen
zich tegenover de bisschop voldoende onafhankelijk op te stellen, maar dat
is dan eerder een gevolg van de bedrijfscultuur die het canonieke systeem
genereert, dan van dwingende normen die tot dat systeem behoren.

Uit wat vooraf gaat blijkt alleszins dat de twee takken van de juridische
dienst die *niet* tot de rechterlijke macht behoren, minder in de greep zijn
van het canonieke beginsel van eenheid van machten. Dat geldt in nog
sterkere mate voor de preventieve cel, die alleen maar adviezen formu-
leert, dan voor de bijzondere procedures die nog wel aardig wat met
rechtspraak te maken hebben. Tegelijk valt op hoe, *naarmate* de afstand
met de eenheid van machten groeit, de contacten met en de invloed van
het profane recht vermeerderen. Er is dus een positieve correlatie tussen
het toenemende contact van de canonieke juridische dienst met de profane
rechtscultuur en de groeiende evolutie in de richting van een systeem van
scheiding van machten. Dat leidt tot de volgende grafische voorstelling.

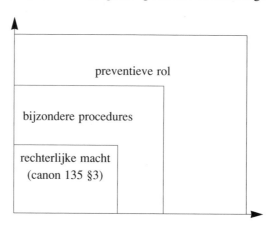

toenemende contacten met
de profane rechtscultuur

preventieve rol

bijzondere procedures

rechterlijke macht
(canon 135 §3)

toenemende scheiding van machten

Het hoeft nauwelijks een betoog dat, op deze manier, de juridische
dienst ook een al te wereldvreemde ontwikkeling van het *ius perfectum*

in de kiem smoort. Een volslagen theologisch gekleurd rechtsconcept wordt in afnemende mate plausibel wanneer de afstand met het strikte gebied van canon 135 §3 groeit.

PRAKTISCHE UITWERKING

Theorieën zijn er om als te theoretisch te worden beschouwd. Is de hier voorgestelde constructie ook praktisch haalbaar? Is zij mogelijk te duur[21]? Slorpt zij niet veel energie op, die op andere vlakken van het kerkelijke leven broodnodig is? Ik meen dat de implementatie best haalbaar is. Vier aandachtspunten staan daarbij vooraan.

1. De juridische dienst wordt diocesaan opgericht, maar niet elk luik ervan blijft noodzakelijk tot één bisdom beperkt.

Het is niet omdat een bisschop een eigen officialaat heeft, een officialaat dat het met geen enkel ander bisdom deelt[22], dat het ook op het niveau van de bijzondere procedures en de preventie *cavalier seul* moet spelen. Het is best mogelijk dat twee of meer verschillende bisdommen exact gelijke bijzondere procedures invoeren met precies dezelfde personeelsleden. Dat laatste zal vaak noodzakelijk zijn, omdat er niet genoeg voldoende onafhankelijke canonisten rondlopen. Men kan immers moeilijk aan een directe medewerker van de bisschop, zoals de officiaal, een sleutelfunctie bij particuliere procedures toekennen. Dat wel doen, zou alvast geen indruk van onafhankelijkheid en onpartijdigheid wekken. Wat geldt op het niveau van de bijzondere procedures, is ook waar voor dat van de preventie. Verschillende diocesen kunnen deze cel als de hunne erkennen. Het voorgaande kan als volgt grafisch worden voorgesteld.

---

[21] Zie over dit probleem ook K. LÜDICKE, *l.c.*, 69.

[22] Een eigen officialaat is de regel, cf. canones 1419-1421. Maar ook interdiocesane rechtbanken zijn mogelijk, cf. canon 1423 § 1. P.A. BONNET, "I tribunali nella loro diversità di grado e di specie", in P.A. BONNET en C. GULLO (ed.), *Il processo matrimoniale canonico*, Vaticaanstad, Libreria Editrice Vaticana, 1994, 197-198; A. MENDONÇA, "The Structural and Functional Aspects of an Appeal Tribunal in Marriage Nullity Cases", *Studia Canonica* 1998, 441-500; A. MENDONÇA, "The Structural and Functional Aspects of an Appeal Tribunal in Marriage Nullity Cases", *Monitor Ecclesiasticus* 1999, 110-196; A. MENDONÇA, "The Functional Aspects of an Appeal Tribunal in Marriage Nullity Cases", *Monitor Ecclesiasticus* 1999, 350-404; M.Á. ORTIZ, "La competenza dei tribunali periferici secondo il grado di giudizio", *Ius Ecclesiae* 1997, 451-482.

R. TORFS

bisdom a	bisdom b	bisdom c	bisdom d	bisdom e	bisdom f	
						}preventie
						}bijzondere procedures
						}officialaat

De volle lijn wijst op gescheiden gremia met gescheiden personeel. Stippellijnen duiden dan weer op instanties die, met hetzelfde personeel en dezelfde procedures, door meer dan een bisdom zijn erkend. Een voorbeeld: bisdom e en f hebben eenzelfde officialaat, delen met drie andere bidommen bijzondere procedures en het bijbehorende personeel, en met twee andere de preventiecel. De juridische dienst van bisdom f bestaat op zichzelf, kan ook met de drie geledingen samen vergaderen, maar dat betekent niet dat alle onderdelen ervan exclusief voor slechts een bisdom werken. Werken ze voor verschillende, dan kan dat per deelgroep van de juridische dienst uiteenlopend zijn.

2. De inhoudelijke uitwerking van de juridische dienst mag niet tegen het universele recht indruisen.

De theoretische betekenis van dit principe houdt weinig geheimen in. Door een lagere wetgever kan geen wet die strijdig is met hoger recht geldig worden uitgevaardigd[23]. Particuliere normen kunnen wel *secundum* en *praeter legem* zijn, maar niet *contra*. Het zuivere bestaan van de juridische dienst lijkt mij in dat verband geen problemen op te leveren. De juridische dienst vult de rechterlijke macht aan, maar dan zó dat het principe van eenheid van machten niet in het gedrang komt. Ook twee van de drie onderdelen die samen de juridische dienst vormen, passen naadloos in het systeem. Dat geldt voor het traditionele officialaat dat gewoon blijft zoals het altijd is geweest. Dat geldt eveneens voor de preventieve cel die als adviesorgaan zonder enige bestuursmacht compleet naast de *trias politica* staat. Alleen bij het uitwerken van bijzondere procedures is het uitkijken geblazen. Vaak zullen zij, *de facto*, een tussenschot zijn tussen het ontstaan van het conflict en het instellen van een hiërarchisch beroep of een strafprocedure. Zelfbinding van de overheid blijft daarbij mogelijk[24]. Zij kan voor zichzelf beslissen om, bijvoorbeeld, geen

---

[23] Zie canon 135 § 2 *in fine*.
[24] R. TORFS, "*Ecclesia Semper Reformanda*: A European Perspective on the Future of the Law, The Journey Ahead", *CLSA Proceedings* 1999, 67-69.

strafprocedure, op te starten zonder prealabele formele stappen te zetten. Maar het tegendeel is allerminst waar. Zo mag een bisschop geen bijkomende vereisten opleggen, bijvoorbeeld het verplichte vatten van een verzoeningscommissie, indien de benadeelde gelovige verkiest om onmiddellijk een hiërarchisch beroep in Rome in te stellen. Zelfs als een bijkomende procedure bedoeld is om de rechtsbescherming van de gelovige alleen maar steviger te maken, mag ze hem het recht niet ontnemen om zijn dossier zo snel als de Codex het mogelijk maakt aan een instantie van de Romeinse curie voor te leggen[25]. Alleen indien de betrokkene de tussenliggende bijzondere procedure volledig vrij aanvaardt, kan zij worden toegepast[26].

Het moge duidelijk zijn dat de inhoudelijke uitwerking van de juridische dienst vooral op het niveau van de bijzondere procedures grote omzichtigheid vereist. Een bijzondere procedure is geen zusje van het privilege. Zelfs als ze de bedoeling heeft voordelen te bieden, mag ze de rechtsgang zoals in de Codex beschreven niet vertragen op een wijze die dwingend is.

3. De juridische dienst wordt niet overbodig gemaakt door het bestaan van interdiocesane juridische diensten. Een goede coördinatie is belangrijk.

Welke zin heeft het per bisdom een juridische dienst te willen organiseren, terwijl heel vaak op het niveau van de bisschoppenconferentie al iets dergelijks bestaat, waarbij de accenten veelal op het profane recht liggen? De voornaamste reden om de in deze bijdrage beschreven juridische dienst in te voeren, ligt erin dat hij de kloof tussen canoniek en profaan recht maximaal beperkt. De aanwezigheid van zowel canonieke als, wellicht, civielrechtelijke expertise op het niveau van het bisdom, leidt tot het formuleren en toepassen van een juridische strategie waarbij de combinatie van het canonieke en het profane recht *ab initio* in de beleidsopties wordt verwerkt. Canonisten en juristen treden met elkaar in gesprek. Op die manier worden ze verplicht zich in de denkwijze en argumentatie van de ander in te leven. En zelfs als in de juridische dienst alleen maar canonisten zitten, zullen ze, bijvoorbeeld in

---

[25] Een dergelijke werkwijze werd ook gevolgd in COMMISSIE JUSTITIA ET PAX NEDERLAND, *Het recht als waarborg. Aanbevelingen tot verbetering van de kerkelijke rechtsgang*, Oegstgeest, Commissie Justitia et Pax Nederland, 1996, 71 p.

[26] Of er op Romeins niveau beroep tegen deze procedures mogelijk is, hangt af van de Heilige Stoel. Zie K. LÜDICKE, *l.c.*, 66.

de preventiecel, willens nillens contacten met de profaanrechtelijke wereld moeten leggen, wat onvermijdelijk een invloed zal hebben op hun denken.

Die integratie wordt, in een configuratie met uitsluitend een verre profaanrechtelijke dienst op het niveau van de bisschoppenconferentie, onvoldoende bereikt. Die dienst krijgt misschien af en toe met de *pathologie* van het juridische beleid op diocesaan niveau af te rekenen, maar verkeert nauwelijks in de mogelijkheid om aan innovatieve denkprocessen te participeren. Dat kan in de diocesane juridische dienst wel. Ook de betrokken canonisten kunnen, zoals gemeld, hun creativiteit botvieren in een vruchtbare dialoog met het profane recht. Ze plooien zich niet terug binnen de, voor de buitenwereld soms ondoorgrondelijke, contouren van het *ius perfectum*.

Uiteraard maakt de in deze bijdrage beschreven juridische dienst de bestaande service op interdiocesaan vlak niet overbodig. Alleen moeten hier heldere afspraken worden gemaakt.

4. De interne organisatie van de juridische dienst combineert eisen *secundum legem* en innovatief denken *praeter legem*.

De gerechtsvicaris moet licentiaat in het canonieke recht en priester zijn (canon 1420 §1). Dit betekent strikt genomen dat één van de drie secties van de juridische dienst, met name de traditionele kerkelijke rechtbank, wordt geleid door de gerechtsvicaris. Moet die ook aan het hoofd staan van de hele juridische dienst? Zeker niet. Niets belet, bijvoorbeeld, dat de globale coördinatie zou berusten bij een leek die profaan jurist is. Er is wel een voorwaarde: de functie van deze persoon mag de concrete autonomie van de gerechtsvicaris in verband met het officialaat niet aantasten. Het leiderschap van het hoofd van de juridische dienst kan slaan op het coördineren van alle diensten, bijvoorbeeld met betrekking tot het organiseren van gemeenschappelijke sessies, en op het effectief besturen van de twee andere diensten, maar de inhoudelijke werking van het officialaat mag hij niet beïnvloeden. De puur praktische werking dan weer wel: hier komen we uit bij de traditionele opdeling officiaal/hoofd van het officialaat zoals die in vele bisdommen bestaat.

Verder belet uiteraard ook niets, en lijkt het mij vaak wenselijk, dat de gerechtsvicaris de leiding neemt van de juridische dienst in zijn geheel. Hij heeft immers heel wat expertise in een binnenkerkelijk milieu opgebouwd.

DE KERKELIJKE RECHTBANK *PRAETER LEGEM*: RUIMERE GEVOLGEN

Bovenstaande beschouwingen tonen aan dat het oprichten van een juridische dienst geen utopie hoeft te blijven. De traditionele rechtbank functioneert in een ruimer geheel, maar behoudt tegelijk haar eigenheid. Het kostenplaatje schrikt niet dadelijk af, want de meeste inspanningen kunnen door een aantal bisdommen samen worden gedaan. Natuurlijk gaat de invoering van de hier voorgestelde constructie niet helemaal vanzelf. Er bestaat trouwens voor kerkleiders geen enkele verplichting om met zoiets als een juridische dienst in zee te gaan. Zij die er niet in geloven, zullen de huidige toestand gegarandeerd blauw blauw laten. De kans dat er voor een *status quo* op het terrein van rechtbanken wordt gekozen, is groot. Waarom? Bisschoppen hebben doorgaans een voorkeur voor pastoraal en geloven minder in structuren. Nochtans verschilt de aanpak hier van land tot land. Nederland en Duitsland zijn een stuk structureler ingesteld dan Frankrijk en België bijvoorbeeld[27]. In de Verenigde Staten bestaat al geruime tijd behoorlijk wat aandacht voor bijzondere procedures[28]. Maar toch, veelal primeert de directe pastoraal. Een andere reden die innovaties op het terrein van het recht belemmert, is precies een doorgedreven, vaak impliciete keuze voor het kerkelijk recht als *ius perfectum* waarin, zie nogmaals canon 1752, het zielenheil de hoogste wet moet zijn. En is het zielenheil met sterk uitgebouwde juridische structuren gebaat? Die werken immers alleen maar individualistische ontsporingen in de hand, zo luidt het vaak.

Tot zover een pleidooi als advocaat van de duivel. Dat recht en pastoraal elkaar niet tegenspreken maar juist bevestigen, is een stelling die hier geen nadere argumentatie behoeft[29]. Een discussie op dit terrein is trouwens vaak steriel en abstract[30]. Daarom even een andere vraag: wat zouden de conse-

---

[27] Nochtans werden met name in Nederland boeiende ideeën over een niet al te structureel uitgebouwd kerkelijk recht ontwikkeld. Zie P. HUIZING en B.A. WILLEMS, "Sacramentele grondslag van kerkrecht", *Tijdschrift voor Theologie* 1976, 244-262.

[28] Zie over successen en problemen V. VONDENBERGER, "Effective Due Process Is Possible in the Church", *Studia Canonica* 1996, 163-176.

[29] Zie de toespraak van paus Johannes Paulus II tot de Romeinse Rota, vooral de nummers 2, 4 en 7, *AAS* 1990, 872-877. Voor commentaar hierop zie T. RINCÓN-PEREZ, "Juridicidad y pastoralidad del Derecho Canónico. Reflexiones a la luz del discurso del Papa a la Rota Romana de 1990", *Ius Canonicum* 1991, 231-252; J. LLOBELL, "I principi del processo canonico: aporia, mimetismo civilistico o esigenza ecclesiale?", *Il Diritto Ecclesiastico* 1996, 125-143.

[30] Vooral de contradictie tussen pastoraal en strafrecht wordt vaak sterk in de verf gezet. Zie hierover V. DE PAOLIS, "L'applicazione della pena canonica", *Monitor Ecclesiasticus* 1989, 70-73.

58 R. TORFS

quenties zijn van de oprichting van een juridische dienst? Het gaat er daarbij niet zozeer om de directe doelstellingen die tot het oprichten ervan leiden nog een keer te formuleren. Veeleer is het nuttig om een aantal eerder indirecte gevolgen kort te analyseren. Ik zie er minstens vier.

1. De uitbouw van een "multicultureel" canoniek recht.

De juridische dienst hanteert, op het vlak van het recht dan, een systeem van *open grenzen*. Het vreemde, *in casu* het profane recht, wordt niet langer gewantrouwd. Het wordt niet meer geassocieerd met dure advocatenrekeningen, wanneer de burcht van het canonieke recht van buiten uit wordt bedreigd. In de nieuwe constructie is vanaf de redactie van particuliere wetteksten het profane recht al in beeld, zij het op bescheiden wijze, namelijk op het weinig spectaculaire niveau van de preventie. Op die manier wordt recht dus *multicultureel*. Met multicultureel doel ik dan niet op een verschil in kleur en smaak dat het locale kerkelijk recht kenmerkt, en dat gebaseerd is op andere volksgewoonten of op uiteenlopende tradities binnen de particuliere kerk. De term *multicultureel* duidt op de integratie tussen twee volkomen verschillende wijzen van omgaan met recht, namelijk de profane methode en het canonieke *ius perfectum*[31]. De centrale vraag is daarbij: hoe kan het kerkelijk recht zijn eigenheid behouden, terwijl het toch in vrede samenleeft met het profane rechtssysteem dat als decor fungeert[32]? De multiculturele samenleving op juridisch vlak.

2. Visitekaartje voor randkerkelijken en niet-kerkelijken.

De juridische dienst doet meer dan alleen binnenkerkelijke conflicten vermijden of ontmijnen. Hij is ook een visitekaartje naar buiten uit. Als de dienst goed is uitgewerkt, de wetgever zijn rol scherp aflijnt tegenover die van profane rechtbanken en duidelijk maakt dat hij geen parallel circuit in het zog van het *privilegium fori* wil creëren, poetst hij het blazoen van de kerk weer op. Randkerkelijken en niet-kerkelijken zullen door een hoogwaardige, transparante juridische dienst waarschijnlijk aangenaam verrast zijn[33].

Vele mensen beschikken vandaag niet meer over een minimale vorming en kennis met betrekking tot religie. Recht daarentegen verschijnt

---

[31] J. LLOBELL, *l.c.*, 143.

[32] Vergelijk met de conclusies van K. LÜDICKE, *l.c.*, 69-70.

[33] De eerste categorie is in theorie betrokken bij de vorming van de publieke opinie in de kerk. De tweede niet. Zie recent over de publieke opinie in de kerk H. SCHWENDENWEIN, "Der Einfluss der öffentlichen Meinungsbildung auf rechtsgestaltende Massnahmen", *De Processibus Matrimonialibus* 1999, 117-144.

te hooi en te gras op de maatschappelijke scène, nu eens als een icoon van individualisme, dan weer als een emancipatoir gegeven. Ieder mens kruist het pad van het recht wel ergens. Welnu, een religie die met een geloofwaardige benadering van recht uitpakt, verhoogt de credibiliteit van haar handelen en zelfs, onrechtstreeks maar onmiskenbaar, van de inhoud van haar gedachtengoed.

3. Een indirecte invloed op het binnenkerkelijke denken.

De externe impulsen die uitgaan van een juridische dienst, kunnen ook een invloed hebben op het denkklimaat in de kerk. Het gevaar van stilstand dat een gesloten systeem bedreigt, ligt niet meer echt op de loer wanneer bijvoorbeeld via een juridische dienst vreemde invloeden binnensijpelen. Onrust en verwarring zijn in de kerk negatieve begrippen. Ze hebben echter ook een positieve keerzijde en heten dan beweging en ideeënrijkdom. Op een ogenblik dat de kerk in vele landen van Europa de neiging heeft getalsmatig af te kalven en de geborgenheid van de eigen niche op te zoeken, biedt de juridische dienst een raam op de buitenwereld. Een blik hierdoor laat zien hoe rust soms op een gebrek aan leven wijst en onrust op een grote vitaliteit. Het recht kleurt dan het leven van de kerk op een wijze die het beperkte juridische kader ruimschoots overstijgt[34].

4. Het veranderende profiel van de kerkjurist.

De oprichting van zoiets als een juridische dienst beïnvloedt het profiel van de kerkjurist. Zolang de meeste praktijkcanonisten uitsluitend het huwelijksrecht beoefenen, blijft het kerkelijk recht een *ius perfectum* tegen wil en dank. De combinatie van enerzijds het beginsel van de onontbindbaarheid van het huwelijk en anderzijds de canonieke nooduitgangen die er desondanks bestaan, leidt vaak tot een beeldvorming die de specialist huwelijks- en huwelijksprocesrecht opvoert als een koorddanser[35]. Hij zit te paard tussen theologie en recht, tussen canonieke

---

[34] Die invloed is vaak positief, maar kan ook negatief zijn. Zie bisschop F. KAMPHAUS, "Was Gott verbunden hat…", geciteerd door N. RUF, *l.c.*, 401: "Mehr als früher ist heute zu prüfen, ob eine Ehe gültig zustande gekommen ist … Der Rechtsweg ist wichtig, das Allheilmittel ist es nicht. Er darf von den Betroffenen nicht mißbraucht werden, indem die Realität dem Recht angepaßt wird."

[35] Sommigen pleiten dienaangaande voor een duidelijker houding. Zie bijvoorbeeld F. DANEELS, "Überlegungen zum kirchlichen Ehenichtigkeitsprozess", *De Processibus Matrimonialibus* 2000, 29: "Weil andererseits der Ausdruck "nichtige Ehe" keineswegs bedeutet, daß nichts gewesen sei, wird nicht geleugnet, daß im Fall einer ungültigen Ehe irgend ein anderes Band als das Eheband bestehen könne. Ich meine jedenfalls, daß wir

eigenheid en algemene rechtstechniek. Een voorbeeld: ongeldige rechts-handelingen zijn ook in het profane recht schering en inslag, maar nietige huwelijken blijven op dat terrein behoorlijk zeldzaam[36]. Een kerke-lijke rechtbank die huwelijken nietig verklaart, fascineert de mensen ongetwijfeld, maar blijft, zeker in Europa, een vorm van omgaan met recht die als hoogst atypisch wordt ervaren.

Voor een goed begrip: de huwelijksrechtspraak heeft ongetwijfeld haar plaats binnen het kerkelijk recht. Ze moet blijven. In de hierboven geformuleerde voorstellen verliest zij allerminst haar betekenis, alleen maar haar exclusiviteit. De andere activiteiten die in het raam van de juridische dienst plaatsvinden, hebben inmiddels een punt gemeen: ze vergen een nauwer contact met het profane recht. Dit betekent meteen ook dat een aankomend kerkjurist in zijn opleiding nood heeft aan een algemeen juridische basisvorming én aan een grondige introductie in de kerk-staat verhoudingen, bekeken vanuit het standpunt van het profane recht. Een cursus over dat laatste onderwerp moet helderheid brengen over de speelruimte en autonomie die kerken, binnen de krijtlijnen van een profaanjuridisch systeem, genieten. Een dergelijke probleemstelling is een logisch gevolg van het verlaten van de *societas perfecta*-gedachte, gecombineerd met de intellectuele moed om aan de bekoring van een alomvattend *ius perfectum* te weerstaan.

Natuurlijk blijft de canonist eerst en vooral een canonist. Hij hoeft niet tegelijk een begenadigd exegeet en als klap op de vuurpijl ook nog eens een scherpzinnig profaan jurist te zijn. Genialiteit is niet meer dan een optie. Wel moet de canonist de beroemde vragenrij – trouwens tevens de titel van een schitterend schilderij van Paul Gauguin – voor ogen houden: *D'où venons-nous? Qui sommes-nous? Où allons-nous?* Voor de eerste vraag is een goed theologisch basisinzicht noodzakelijk. De meeste kerkleiders en canonisten zijn het, met betrekking tot de noodzaak hiervan, eens. *Qui sommes-nous?* slaat dan weer op het zelfverstaan van de canonist. Hier geldt het principe dat een kerkjurist steeds zijn eigen positie en functioneren in vraag moet stellen. Altijd dus, en niet alleen in periodes van crisis, ofschoon dat de laatste veertig, vijftig jaar op hetzelfde neerkomt. De derde vraag, *où allons-nous?*, heeft (ook, niet uitsluitend) te maken met de rol van het pro-

---

zweideutige Formulierungen bei der Vorstellung der Ehenichtigkeitsverfahren vermeiden und klar zum Ausdruck bringen müssen, daß sich diese Eheverfahren auf das Bestehen oder Nichtbestehen des Ehebandes von Anfang an beziehen."

[36] Zie over de nietigheid van rechtshandelingen het klassieke werk van O. ROBLEDA, *La nulidad del Acto Jurídico*, Rome, Libreria Editrice dell'Università Gregoriana, 1964, viii + 358 p.

fane recht bij het in de praktijk brengen van het kerkelijk recht. De canonist moet weten, of weten hoe hij kan te weten komen, wat de profaanjuridische kwaliteit en consequenties van zijn functioneren zijn.

Een modern canonist dient, vanaf zijn vorming, de draad met het profane rechtsdenken weer op te nemen. Wie als kerkjurist een reële band met de wereld van het profane recht wantrouwig tegemoet blikt of ronduit onwenselijk vindt, bewijst daardoor paradoxaal genoeg dat hij op theologisch vlak de boot heeft gemist. Een vijand van het profane recht verbergt immers achter een schijnbaar pastorale bewogenheid een diep heimwee naar de *societas perfecta*.

SLOTBESCHOUWINGEN

Bovenstaand verhaal gaat over kerkelijke rechtbanken. Het kan op twee niveaus worden gelezen.

Op een eerste niveau wordt duidelijk dat het universele recht het facet *rechtspraak* als derde luik en sluitstuk van de *trias politica* onvoldoende tot ontwikkeling laat komen. Een remedie bestaat erin om naast de horizontale lijn van de drie machten ook een verticale te trekken. Hoe? Via de oprichting van de juridische dienst, die naast de traditionele kerkelijke rechtbank ook de bijzondere procedures en de preventieve cel omvat. De juridische dienst zorgt voor een structurele meerwaarde, voor een geloofwaardiger kerk, voor een contactpunt met de profane samenleving.

Op een tweede niveau houdt de oprichting van de juridische dienst ook een *statement* in. Een *statement* kan een reden zijn om iets wat in wezen positief is, toch niet tot stand te brengen. Waarover gaat het? Over een positieve keuze voor een kerk die niet langer een *societas perfecta* is en die dus complexloos bepaalde profaanrechtelijke verworvenheden verwelkomt. Vervolgens zou zij aan de verleiding moeten weerstaan om de *societas perfecta* door een *ius perfectum*, het zich terugtrekken op een subcultureel eiland met eigen wetmatigheden, te vervangen. In die zin impliceert het instellen van een juridische dienst ook theologische keuzes. Het verlaten van de *societas perfecta* gedachte tijdens Vaticanum II wordt op het niveau van het particuliere kerk canoniek geconcretiseerd. En tegelijk houdt de juridische dienst een boodschap in naar de toekomst toe: de dialoog met de profane wereld is geen vluchtig modeverschijnsel uit de jaren zestig van de vorige eeuw. Het canonieke recht heeft open grenzen en opteert voor een multiculturele juridische cultuur. Dat is spannend, maakt wat onrustig, schept een beetje verwarring, maar blijft ten diepste wezenlijk katholiek.

CHURCH TRIBUNALS *SECUNDUM* AND *PRAETER LEGEM*

RIK TORFS

The glorious days of the *societas perfecta* are gone[1]. It would hardly enter anyone's head to describe the church in this way now. So does this mean that all we now have is the church as *communio*, as the People of God or the Body of Christ? When it comes to official speeches and theological reflections that often seems to be the case. However, and what I am saying is nothing new, *societas perfecta* thinking is not dead[2]. Is this because structures are stronger than ideas? Perhaps. But that is not the only reason. For sometimes the opposite is true and ideas are stronger than structures, as the political expression of the ideas of the Enlightenment in a number of countries has proven.

There is also another reason why the shadow of the *societas perfecta* still hangs over canon law, and it is this: there is no immediately visible alternative. It is all very well, a church as a *communio*, but how does it work under canon law? Surely there must be more than a legal outline of the *absence* of the old model? Or is there such a thing as 'negative canon law'? These questions are extremely interesting. Perhaps too interesting for a canonist. So I will not ask them. I would prefer to begin with a simple description, not of possible new norms *de lege ferenda*, but of the difficult exodus from the *societas perfecta* idea. How does man free himself from something which he does not like but cannot do without? I will deal with this question first, along with all the consequences associated with the problem, including missed opportunities and unexpected difficulties. So, from a description of the current climate of thought, I arrive at the church tribunal. Can it have a significant part to play within the church at the present time? A part different from its current one? And if so, what part, and how?

---

[1] P. GRANFIELD, "The Rise and Fall of Societas Perfecta", *Concilium* 1982, n° 7, 3-9.

[2] R. TORFS, "The Roman Catholic Church and Secular Legal Culture in the Twentieth Century", *Studia Historiae Ecclesiasticae* 1999, 1-20.

EXODUS FROM *SOCIETAS PERFECTA* THINKING

What do bishops, canon lawyers and administrators do, who have always tacitly been active within a *societas perfecta* and suddenly hear that the underlying theological presuppositions are not quite right? In the worst case, they wait for their retirement. Usually, however, they will look for a way out which integrates the new ideas without having to change their *modus vivendi* entirely. In very practical terms this has led to a way of working on two levels within the church.

One possible first reaction to the decline of the *societas perfecta* idea consists of limiting it *ratione materiae*. What this actually means is the ecclesiastical authorities thinking and acting just as autonomously as they did before. The *territory* within which this independent existence plays itself out is, however, smaller than before, and it is more closely connected to that which is religious and spiritual in the strict sense. In short, the church remains just as autonomous as before, but the playing-field is more restricted. This approach can be put into practice in various different ways. For example by focusing more on areas of canon law which are specifically religious, such as sacramental law or liturgical law. There is an impression that more top canonists are working on questions in precisely these sectors. Quite rightly, of course, and with considerable success, when I think of authors such as John Huels[3]. At the same time however, anyone who works on this type of material probably will not be affected by the accusation that he is involved in legally ordering a parallel society. Sometimes this brings us to what could be called a *ius perfectum*[4]. The church is not, perhaps, a perfect society standing by itself. The law which it promulgates and applies, however, has a completely different dynamism to secular law. It is friendlier, gentler, more pastoral, correcting its own hardness when appropriate. This raises the following question: although the *ius perfectum* creates an autonomous field of activity in a way that is not so very different from the *societas perfecta*, the discourse is more modest. Canon law is no longer revealed as a rival to secular law. Anyway, rivalry is an ugly word. Canon law stands for gentle values. It is as soft as silk. That is more or less the underlying, implicit idea. The reality, of

---

[3] See for example J.M. HUELS, *More Disputed Questions in Liturgy*, Chicago, Liturgy Training Publications, 1996, vi + 200 p.; J.M. HUELS, "Principles of Liturgical Adaptation in Light of Justice and Forgiveness", *CLSA Proceedings* 1999, 1-25.

[4] R. TORFS, *l.c.*, 13-14.

course, is more complex. It is not, for example, because sacraments have a solid theological basis that it is impossible to deal with them in a hard, juridical way.

There was also some apparent modesty in discussion of canon law during the period between the Council and the Code, when rather exotic experiments were the order of the day. The term *penal law* was not so popular at the time, as *disciplinary law* seemed more modest. In this way, once again, there was an implicit distancing from a *societas perfecta* context. That is because disciplinary law is the law of a particular sub-group, such as a professional association or a sporting federation, within a broader and generally acknowledged social context. The *societas perfecta* is abandoned by limiting the *field of activity* of ecclesiastical autonomy. Within that field of activity the church applies a law which is entirely its own, a kind of *ius perfectum*. On just one occasion has that *ius perfectum* caught on with secular lawyers. That was in the case of *latae sententiae* penalties. Something very strange was happening here. In the ninth of the ten principles approved by the General Meeting of the Synod of Bishops in 1967 as the most important principles that should underlie the new code of canon law[5], it was insisted that *latae sententiae* penalties should be eliminated as far as possible. At the same time, progressive secular lawyers found this legal concept refreshing: it meant the criminal was being taken seriously. He was held responsible for the analysis and evaluation of his own crime. For a while, a strange connection came into being between *latae sententiae* penalties and the permissive society. Only for a while, of course: in most cases the *ius perfectum* was not suitable for export.

The second possible reaction in the area of canon law goes one step further. Here the ecclesiastical authorities do not withdraw exclusively to familiar religious terrain. The code of canon law, the legislative activities of the legislature, the scope for the activities of the canon

---

[5] "Principia quae codicis iuris canonici recognitionem dirigant", *Communicationes* 1969, 84-85:

"De recognoscendo iure poenali

9. In recognitione iuris poenalis Ecclesiae, principium reducendi poenas in Codice stabilitas, nemo est qui non acceptet. Verum suppressionem omnium poenarum ecclesiasticarum, cum ius coactivum, cuiuslibet societatis perfectae proprium, ab Ecclesia abiudicari nequeat, nemo canonistarum admittere videtur.

Mens est ut poenae generatim sint ferendae sententiae et in solo foro externo irrogentur et remittantur. Quod ad poenas latae sententiae attinet, etsi a non paucis earum abolitio proposita sit, mens est ut illae ad paucos omnino casus reducantur, imo ad paucissima eaque gravissima delicta."

lawyer do not immediately shrink. Canon law activities, even if they look very secular, are simply classified differently and given a different name. Zenon Grocholewski[6], for example, emphasises that so-called "administrative" conflicts also have a spiritual dimension[7].

The heart of this matter can be illustrated by a story told by German canonist Norbert Ruf a few years ago[8]. An archpriest from the Russian Uniate Church was summoned before the *Landgericht* in Freiburg charged with an indecency offence. Prior to this, however, penal procedures under canon law had already taken place before the church tribunal in Freiburg, brought by the Congregation for the Doctrine of the Faith. The archpriest's solicitor asked the secular court to call the judicial vicar as a witness. The latter, however, invoked his capacity as a pastor of souls, as a result of which he would not have to testify according to German law. A judicial vicar as a pastor of souls? How could that be, wondered the secular court. The judicial vicar replied in Latin: *salus animarum in Ecclesia suprema semper lex esse debet*, from the closing sentence of canon 1752. The secular court, and later the appeal court, were satisfied with this explanation. As for the archpriest, he was condemned to a two-year prison sentence. Not, of course, *because* the judicial vicar was a pastor of souls, although he did not have to testify for precisely that reason.

Not only does the judicial vicar act as a pastor of souls, however, but so does the ordinary ecclesiastical judge, according to the description by Karl-Heinz Selge[9]. Selge distinguishes between *cura animarum* and *cura pastoralis*, whereby the latter is broader and implies the care of souls. From the well-known canon 517 §2 which deals with pastoral care in a parish with a shortage of priests, it emerges that the laity can also exercise pastoral care, i.e. *a fortiori* the care of souls. Selge also explains

---

[6] Z. GROCHOLEWSKI, "De ordinatione ac munere tribunalium in ecclesia ratione quoque habita iustitiae administrativae", *Ephemerides Iuris Canonici* 1992, 75.

[7] See also the study by A.J.T. VAN DEN HOUT, *L'ecclesialità del processo contenzioso-ordinario e del contenzioso-amministrativo*, Rome, Pontificium Athenaeum Sanctae Crucis, 1998, 330 p.

[8] N. RUF, "Zum pastoralen Standort des Diözesangerichtes", in R. PUZA and A. WEIß (ed.), *Iustitia in caritate. Festgabe für Ernst Rößler zum 25jährigen Dienstjubiläum als Offizial der Diözese Rottenburg-Stuttgart*, in E. GÜTHOFF and K.-H. SELGE (ed.), *Adnotationes in ius canonicum*, III, Frankfurt am Main/Berlin/Bern/New York/Paris/Vienna, Peter Lang, 1997, 396-405.

[9] K.-H. SELGE, "Der kirchliche Richter als Seelsorger im ordentlichen Ehenichtigkeitsverfahren erster Instanz", in E. GÜTHOFF en K.-H. SELGE (ed.), *Festgabe F.X. Walter zur Vollendung des 65. Lebensjahres*, Fredersdorf, Rodak, 1994, 31.

very well why the office of ecclesiastical judge is an office involving the care of souls. His reasoning is as follows: insofar as the judge, through his jurisprudence, helps to realise the immediate local care of souls, he is exercising the *indirect* or mediate care of souls. Although jurisdiction is also a pastoral service, the judge is not automatically involved in the care of souls in the strict sense. He does, however, act as a pastor of souls if he carries out tasks during the procedures which are related to the care of individual souls. Here his care of souls is *immediate*, although his judicial office is only partly linked to the care of souls. That is because the principal task is to organise the competent professional conduct of procedure. His office is therefore not a monofunctional, but a multifunctional pastoral one. These facets come to the fore, for example, when the judge gives personal advice or offers practical notes on the procedures[10].

Ruf's story and Selge's well-constructed reasoning demonstrate how even in procedural law – not a particularly animated branch of law, and one which requires considerable technical skills – a purely juridical approach is called into question. The man passing judgment is a pastor.

It becomes clear how a different approach to law, a kind of *ius perfectum* thinking, is increasingly colouring canon law. The new, apparently gentler, vision of the law is not limited to typically ecclesiastical sectors such as liturgical law, teaching office or sacramental law. It also transforms administrative procedure, turning the judge into a pastor of souls. In short, the whole territory of the old *societas perfecta* is gradually being conquered by the *ius perfectum*[11].

There are areas of tension behind the official image. On the one hand there is a certain tension between the care of souls and passing judgment as a judge, certainly in specific cases. What is more, the search for the truth and strict procedural law cannot always be combined without difficulty. Certainly not in practice. The formalism which can never be completely avoided in procedural terms, sometimes jeopardises the care of souls and to some extent also the truth[12]. A procedural error that results

---

[10] K.-H. SELGE, *l.c.*, 41.

[11] Here is another example. The rights and obligations of all Christian believers seem to be very similar to human rights in secular society. This, however, is only apparent. Due to theological and ecclesiological thinking, the difference is significant. See J. HERRANZ CASADO, "Renewal and Effectiveness in Canon Law", *Studia Canonica* 1994, 5-31.

[12] Similar tensions can be seen in the debate on the question of whether procedural law should defend the subjective right or the objective right. See F. ROBERTI, *De processibus*, Rome, Pontificium Institutum Utriusque Iuris, 1941, p. 73-74, n° 26: "Omnes

in a judgment being null and void[13] although it is incontrovertibly in accordance with the truth in terms of material law, is an interesting illustration of this. Procedural law is often too hard for those who are pastors and too convoluted for those looking for the truth[14].

Let us return, however, to the exodus from the world of the *societas perfecta*. This is not particularly characterised by the implicit demand for structures that correspond to theological innovations. A more important question is: how can a traditional, highly autonomous operational method remain in force if the church as *societas perfecta* cannot continue to act as the underlying basis for it? The escape route has initially consisted of a *ratione materiae* retreat to familiar terrain which has a theological colouring, and this has happened via a *ius perfectum*. The second stage is for the theologically coloured *ius perfectum* approach to influence the whole legal system.

The working method outlined here, both in its first, more tentative version and in its second, rather more daring form, is manifestly defensive. The canonist is retrenching. Since he no longer wishes to uphold the semblance of a legal framework for the *societas perfecta*, he becomes a highly theologically inspired canonist, even a pastor of souls. This entails consequences. In a social context in which the law is absolutely omnipresent, the canonist becomes an amateur in the legal domain. He acts within clearly defined outlines and follows the specific logic of canon law. If the canonist's approach collides with secular law, expensive secular lawyers need to be brought in to salvage whatever remains. They may, for example, point out that a proper understanding of the freedom of religion also requires a good deal of autonomy for churches. Many bishops attach more significance to the views of the secular lawyer defending them *ad extra* than to the opinion of the canonist, who is never a dangerous opponent. In a specifically ecclesiastical context he can always be neutralised completely legally.

moderni doctores finem processus iuris actuationem statuunt; inter se autem non conveniunt cum agitur de statuendo proprio eius fine. Etenim plures affirmant processum formaliter ordinari ad exsecutionem iuris obiectivi seu legis, indirecte vero tueri iura subiectiva. Alii contra contendunt finem proximum esse exsecutionem iuris subiectivi, ex qua indirecte etiam ius obiectivum exsecutioni mandatur."

[13] On certain aspects of this question see M. THÉRIAULT, "The Nullity of Some Processual Acts in Light of Canon 124", *Forum* 1994, n° 1, 29-42.

[14] Of course there is absolutely n° contradiction between *iustitia* and *veritas* at the theoretical level. On this subject see Z. GROCHOLEWSKI, "Iustitia ecclesiastica et veritas", *Periodica* 1995, 7-30.

I have considerable difficulties with this approach, however, mainly because of two reasons which can doubtless be translated into theological terms, but do not in essence form part of theology.

The first reason is the melancholy and hopelessness associated with a defensive strategy. Those who only defend their boundaries, their possessions, their legal position, are not building. What is more, remarkably enough, after a time there arises a growing impression that what is being defended is not something quite legitimate, but a privilege. This is the impression that sometimes exists in relation to the defence of Fortress Europe. Suspicion then emerges. Anyone who absolutely wants to keep something, probably thinks that he will not succeed in legitimately acquiring a similar thing in future. If it should ever disappear, what he has now will never return.

But there is more. In view of the rich tradition of canon law, and the influence that it has had on secular law, it is shameful to have to observe that it should now, for theological reasons, choose an approach to law which is no longer really relevant to society in general. If a theological approach to canon law means that it is not really law any more, but a formal legitimation of dominant theological thinking, that is a very high price to pay. Can and must anything be done about this defensive attitude and legal-technical abdication? That is the question that then arises.

I think something can and must be done. One factor that is underestimated by church leaders is the ominous thought that a strategic withdrawal *ratione materiae* or in the methodological domain does not mean that the secular courts will continue to refrain from intervening in internal church affairs. Monsignor Ruud Huysmans spoke about this at the occasion of the biannual study gathering of the Working Group of Dutch-Speaking Canonists (WNC) in December 2000: our own canon law hardly has any part to play in problems that affect the secular society, such as civil liability in cases of sexual abuse[15]. Of course this idea seems surprising at first sight: the church is occupying less ground, or doing so in a different way from when it was still presenting itself as *societas perfecta*, hence it seems to be less ambitious, and yet it faces more interventions from secular courts than before. This can, of course, only be the case if the strategic withdrawal by the church is accompanied by an increasingly expansive system of secular law, a system of secular law that is occupying more territory and becoming more forceful in its regulation.

---

[15] R.G.W. HUYSMANS, "Geen rol kerkrecht in kwestie aansprakelijkheid bisschop", *1 2 1* 2000, 695-696.

THE LINK TO MODERN SOCIETY

For some people the progressive juridicalisation of modern society is an unfortunate illustration of all-pervasive individualism. Too many rights and no obligations. The lament is well-known. Although there are some excesses, however, the emancipatory aspect of law should also not be forgotten. Since the Second World War, for example, human rights have resulted in real liberation, that was difficult to find in the time of National Socialism. In short, despite the risk of excesses, a well-structured code of canon law can form a valuable point of contact between the church and the world. Within this pioneering function of law in general, the role of the tribunals and their jurisprudence seems to be particularly important. With just a little exaggeration it is possible to say that the future of canon law depends on whether or not the tribunals work. If a norm at that level cannot be analysed and interpreted, it will remain a simple manifesto statement, and it will appear to be primarily ideological at the expense of legal effectiveness.

One problem at present is that the church tribunals are absent in certain areas. I am certainly not trying to say that most church tribunals are not functioning well. Quite the opposite is true. They are, however, struggling with a double handicap. They are operating in a system where there is no separation of powers or balance of powers. And they are involved virtually exclusively in marriage-related cases. This double handicap, however, may well be less double than it seems: it is precisely *because* the separation of powers in the church is not accepted, that not much is left to the tribunal other than the law of marriage, which is very important in pastoral terms, but relatively unimportant in terms of church policy. Not much can be achieved in other areas. This is because the tribunals are not sufficiently independent.

Can things be different? I will leave all *de lege ferendae* solutions aside for a moment. I will also set aside quality requirements for the process of canon law, as Salvatore Berlingò formulated them back in 1993[16]. Berlingò referred to three requirements, of which the publication of the acts for the parties and the real technical right of defence are achievable today. His third point, the clear distinction between the parties and the decision-making body as well as the independence of the

---

[16] S. BERLINGÒ, "Il diritto al 'processo' (can. 221 § 2 CIC) in alcune procedure particolari", *Persona y Derecho. Suplemento 'Fidelium iura' de derecho y deberes fundamentales del fiel* 1993, 339-358, i.c. 354-357.

tribunal, is already more sensitive. In order to make it truly concrete, a form of separation of powers is needed. In many people's eyes, however, there is a theological basis for the absence of this. The dream of an independent ecclesiastical court must not, therefore, be considered to be a reality that can be achieved quickly.

What is acceptable in terms of canon law and would be achievable, with good will, is a construction in particular law, whereby the church tribunal is included in a more comprehensive legal department[17]. Of course canon 135 §3 must always be borne in mind: judicial power, which is held by judges or judicial colleges, must be exercised in the way prescribed by law, and cannot be delegated, except to perform acts preparatory to some decree or sentence. Problems in that area could, in my opinion, be prevented by perceiving the legal department more broadly than as exclusively an organ of the judicial power[18]. That judicial power plays a double role, and is a pivotal factor in the proposal. It continues to be one of the three powers mentioned in canon 135 §1[19]. At the same time it forms a central part of the legal department which is to be set up. As regards the legislative, executive and judicial power, the structure is just as it was.

three powers {	legislation	executive power	
			jurisdiction

Jurisdiction represents one of the three powers, but *de iure* administrative tribunals do not exist at the diocesan level and *de facto* ordinary disputes are hardly ever brought before them. At the most there is – and the situation differs here from one country to another – a *revival*

---

[17] The legal department relates to the scope and room for manoeuvre that are available to canon law. Of course other points will also continue to be important, such as the improved functioning, efficient organisation and critical self-evaluation of the ecclesiastical court. On this subject see, inter alia, M.A. HACK, "Selected Issues in the Administration of a Diocesan Tribunal (Everything They Don't Teach in Canon Law Class)", *CLSA Proceedings* 1996, 187-209.

[18] A broader conception is, of course, also possible within the judicial power, for example by extending the existing possibilities under particular law, or through better utilisation of what already exists. On these and other matters see the very creative article by K. LÜDICKE, "Möglichkeit und Notwendigkeit einer partikularrechtlichen kirchlichen Gerichtsbarkeit in Deutschland", *De Processibus Matrimonialibus* 1999, 55-70.

[19] E. CORECCO, "Nature et structure de la *sacra potestas* dans la doctrine et dans le nouveau code de droit canonique", *Revue de droit canonique* 1984, 389 sees the simple fact of this division into three powers as a regrettable theological regression.

of the penal trial. It is also for this reason that in a graphical representation of the *trias politica* within the church, jurisdiction covers a more limited field than legislation and the executive power.

What services, other than the traditional tribunal, should be offered by a future legal department? It would probably have to bring together existing specific procedures, whether they are aimed at conflict avoidance such as diocesan reconciliation agencies set up in the context of canon 1733 or whether they introduce special procedures, for example in cases of sexual abuse or cases relating to the freedom of theologians to express their opinions. Are these bodies independent or do they form part of judicial power in the sense of canon 135 §3? That entirely depends on how the relevant particular norms are drawn up, although the bishop can make commitments to some extent, but on the other hand he cannot definitively transfer the rights conferred upon him by canon 381.

A last section of the legal department can be identified in the area of prevention work. The drafting of general statutes or specific contracts to keep conflicts at bay certainly forms part of this. There will certainly be points of contact with secular law, so that the formal involvement or structural cooperation on the part of secular lawyers will be necessary. All this leads to the next diagram.

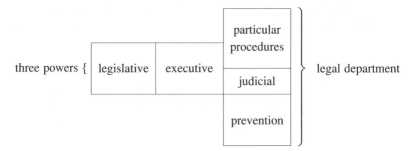

It is noticeable that the traditional judicial power is the pivotal point where the horizontal axis (the three powers) and the vertical axis (the legal department) meet. The legal department also corrects the imperfection of the horizontal axis by further extending the judicial power which is limited in scope. What the traditional judicial power does *not* offer in terms of procedures can be absorbed by the specific procedures. At the same time, specific procedures can also be created that do not belong to the judicial power. In my opinion there is room for external arbitration here.

The proposed construction appears to be reasonably obvious, but it will make a deeper impact on the system than a superficial observer might suspect. That is because the legal department brings secular law closer to canon law once again. The judicial power appears to be weakened by the purely ecclesiastical approach: since there is no balance of powers, jurisprudence only covers a fraction of the ground that is covered by legislation and the administration. The complementing that does take place is *praeter legem*. The special procedures which are involved here are less typical of the church than the universal norms. They are structured at the local level, and the influence and implicit demands of the secular legal culture will never be far away. The unity of powers is probably also subject to amendment. In a specific procedure seeking to achieve general credibility in society, it is impossible to emphasise the bishop as the highest judge. It is counter-productive even to refer to this idea. This kind of approach will probably create a suspicious mood, while the role of the bishop as defined in universal law also remains in place if specific procedures do not explicitly refer to it.

To put it differently: a specific procedure does not withdraw itself *de iure* from the principle of unity of powers as expressed indirectly, for example, in canon 381[20]. *De facto*, however, that principle has been found not to be psychologically feasible. It is not feasible, and it is probably not what is intended. A bishop who initiates a specific procedure is not obliged to do so. The decision to initiate such a procedure implies a certain willingness on the part of the bishop to distribute powers. That willingness cannot be fully honoured in structural terms: if he is not willing at a later stage to submit to the outcome of 'power-sharing' procedures which he has initiated, he probably cannot be forced to do so. In that case, however, we are already in the area of enforcement. When working out the specific procedure an ultimate will to reserve judgment can never be emphasised.

In the case of the *prevention* activities of the legal department, the approach to the world of secular law is even closer. Prevention work, of course, involves the avoidance of conflicts within the church. On the other hand it is also important to keep areas of tension with the secular society to a minimum. Prevention work in this domain involves investigating possible consequences of policies of the bishop and his policy institutions in secular law. This does not have to lead to a slavish following of social fashions and trends. It is useful, however, to weigh and

---

[20] This is because *potestas* in canon 381 § 1 is seen as *potestas regiminis*. See G. BIER, in *Münsterischer Kommentar zum CIC*, Essen, Ludgerus, since 1985 (loose-leaf; version: 33.Erg.Lfg.Juni 2000), 381, 6.

assess the possible consequences in secular law of the church policy
beforehand. A few possible questions: does the secular judge intervene
if the bishop makes decisions without following the procedure prescribed within the church? Is the bishop liable in civil law for the actions
of his priests? For *all* actions? Of *all* his priests? If the answer to some
of those questions may sound rather disturbing, it is up to the bishop to
ascertain what possible 'prophetic' action may cost him. This then falls
under the heading of canon law and economics. In any case, since the
prevention task is limited to providing recommendations, it is normally
not burdened by the principle of unity of powers. It may be that the
providers of prevention measures do not succeed in maintaining sufficient independence from the bishop due to *metus reverentialis*, but that
is rather a result of the operational culture generated by the system of
canon law than of the compulsory norms forming part of that system.

In any case it is clear from the above that the two branches of the
legal department which do *not* belong to the judicial power are less
affected by the principle of the unity of powers in canon law. This is
even more applicable in the case of the prevention group which only
makes recommendations, than in the case of the special procedures
which have a significant involvement in jurisdiction. At the same time it
is noticeable how, *as* the distance from the unity of powers grows, con-
tacts with and the influence of secular law increase. Hence there is a
positive correlation between the increasing contact between the legal
department under canon law and the secular legal culture and the growing development towards a system of division of powers. That leads to
the following graphical representation.

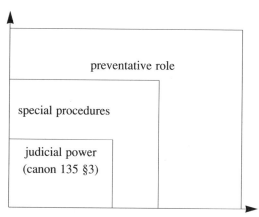

increasing contact with
secular legal culture

preventative role

special procedures

judicial power
(canon 135 §3)

increasing separation of powers

It scarcely needs to be said that in this way the legal department will also nip in the bud any development of a *ius perfectum* which is too alien to the world. A concept of law which is fully theological in its colouring becomes less plausible as the distance from the strict scope of canon 135 §3 increases.

PRACTICAL OUTWORKING

Theories are there to be considered too theoretical. Is the construction presented here feasible in practice too? Could it be too expensive[21]? Will it not absorb too much energy which is desperately needed in other areas of church life? I consider implementation to be perfectly feasible. There are four points that will require attention here.

1. The legal department is structured at the diocesan level, but not all of its sections are necessarily restricted to a single diocese.

Just because a diocese has its own officialate, which it does not share with any other diocese[22], it still does not have to act on its own when it comes to special procedures and prevention. It is perfectly possible for two or more different dioceses to introduce exactly identical special procedures using precisely the same personnel. This will often be necessary, since there are not enough sufficiently independent canonists in circulation. It is difficult to give a direct member of the bishop's staff, such as the judicial vicar, a key role in specific procedures. To do so probably would not give an impression of independence and impartiality. What is true at the level of special procedures is also true in the area of prevention. A number of dioceses can acknowledge this group as their own. The above can be graphically represented as follows.

---

[21] On this problem see also K. LÜDICKE, *l.c.*, 69.

[22] An officialate of its own is the rule, cf. canones 1419-1421. Interdiocesan courts are also possible, cf. canon 1423 § 1. P.A. BONNET, "I tribunali nella loro diversità di grado e di specie", in P.A. BONNET en C. GULLO (ed.), *Il processo matrimoniale canonico*, Vatican City, Libreria Editrice Vaticana, 1994, 197-198; A. MENDONÇA, "The Structural and Functional Aspects of an Appeal Tribunal in Marriage Nullity Cases", *Studia Canonica* 1998, 441-500; A. MENDONÇA, "The Structural and Functional Aspects of an Appeal Tribunal in Marriage Nullity Cases", *Monitor Ecclesiasticus* 1999, 110-196; A. MENDONÇA, "The Functional Aspects of an Appeal Tribunal in Marriage Nullity Cases", *Monitor Ecclesiasticus* 1999, 350-404; M.Á. ORTIZ, "La competenza dei tribunali periferici secondo il grado di giudizio", *Ius Ecclesiae* 1997, 451-482.

						}prevention
						}special procedures
						}officialate
diocese a	diocese b	diocese c	diocese d	diocese e	diocese f	

The solid line points to separate bodies with separate personnel. Dotted lines, on the other hand, refer to bodies with the same personnel and the same procedures which are recognised by more than one diocese. Here is an example: dioceses e and f have the same officialate, share special procedures and the associated personnel with three other dioceses and the prevention group with two others. The legal department of diocese f exists in its own right, and can also bring its three parts together for a meeting, but that does not mean that all its parts work exclusively for a single diocese. If they work for different ones, this may be different for each sub-group of the legal department.

2. The substantial outworking of the legal department must not infringe universal law.

There is nothing very mysterious about the theoretical significance of this principle. A lower legislator cannot validly promulgate a law that is contrary to a higher law[23]. Particular norms may be *secundum* and *praeter legem*, but not *contra*. The simple existence of the legal department does not seem to me to raise any problems in that connection. The legal department supplements the judicial power, but does so in such a way that the principle of unity of powers is not jeopardised. Two of the three components that jointly form the legal department also fit seamlessly into the system. That is true of the traditional officialate, which simply remains as it has always been. It also applies to the prevention group which is a complete advisory body with no power of governance alongside the *trias politica*. It is only when working out special procedures that there is a need to sound a note of caution. These will often, *de facto*, be an intermediate stage between the emergence of the conflict and the bringing of a hierarchical appeal or penal procedures. It is always possible for the authorities to make its own commitments in

---

[23] See canon 135 § 2 *in fine*.

this area[24]. They may, for example, decide that they will not initiate penal procedures without taking certain formal preliminary steps. The opposite, however, is certainly not true. Hence a bishop cannot impose additional requirements, for example the obligatory calling of a reconciliation commission, if the injured believer chooses to submit a hierarchical appeal in Rome immediately. Even if an additional procedure is intended to create greater legal protection for the believer, it cannot deprive him of the right to present his case as quickly as is allowed by the Code, to an institution of the Roman curia[25]. The intervening special procedure can only be used if the person in question accepts it completely freely[26].

It should be clear that working out the substantial aspects of the legal department requires a great deal of circumspection, particularly with regard to special procedures. A special procedure is not really a privilege. Even if it is intended to provide benefits, it must not delay the legal procedure as described in the Code in any way that is compulsory.

3. The legal department is not made superfluous by the existence of inter-diocesan legal departments. Proper coordination is important.

What is the point of seeking to organise a legal department for each diocese, while such a thing very often already exists at the level of the Conference of Bishops, where the emphasis is mainly on secular law? The main reason for introducing the legal department described here is that it keeps the gulf between canon and secular law as narrow as possible. The presence of both canon and probably civil law expertise within the diocese leads to the formulation and implementation of a legal strategy in which the combination of canon and secular law is incorporated in the policy options *ab initio*. Canonists and lawyers enter into discussion with each other. In this way each group is obliged to empathise with the way in which the other thinks and argues. Even if the legal department consists entirely of canonists, they will, for example in the prevention group, have contact with the world of secular law whether they like it or not, and this will inevitably influence the way they think.

[24] R. TORFS, *"Ecclesia Semper Reformanda*: A European Perspective on the Future of the Law, The Journey Ahead", *CLSA Proceedings* 1999, 67-69.

[25] A similar working method was also followed in COMMISSIE JUSTITIA ET PAX NEDERLAND, *Het recht als waarborg. Aanbevelingen tot verbetering van de kerkelijke rechtsgang*, Oegstgeest, Commissie Justitia et Pax Nederland, 1996, 71 p.

[26] Whether an appeal is possible in Rome against this procedures, depends on the Holy See. See K. LÜDICKE, *l.c.*, 66.

This integration is not sufficiently achieved in a configuration with only a distant secular legal department at the level of the Conference of Bishops. That department may occasionally be able to deal with *pathological* situations in the legal department at diocesan level, but it is hardly possible for it to participate in innovative thinking processes at all. This is, however, possible in the diocesan legal department. The canonists involved can, as been stated, also give free rein to their creativity in a fruitful dialogue with secular lawyers. Then they will not draw back into the contours, sometimes impenetrable to the outside world, of the *ius perfectum*.

Of course the legal department described in this essay does not make the existing department at inter-diocesan level superfluous. Clear commitments need to be made here.

4. The internal organisation of the legal department combines demands *secundum legem* and innovative thinking *praeter legem*.

The judicial vicar must be a licentiate in canon law and also a priest (canon 1420 §1). Strictly speaking this means that one of the three sections of the legal department, namely the traditional ecclesiastical tribunal, is led by the judicial vicar. Must he also lead the entire legal department? Certainly not. There is nothing, for example, to prevent the overall coordination from being carried out by a layperson who is a secular lawyer. There is one condition, however: the position of this person must not infringe the specific autonomy of the judicial vicar in connection with the officialate. The leadership provided by the head of the legal department may involve the coordination of all departments, for example in relation to the organisation of joint sessions, and the effective guidance of the two other services, but he must not influence the content of the activities of the officialate. He may, however, influence the practical aspects of its operations: this brings us to the traditional division between the judicial vicar and the head of the officialate which exists in many dioceses.

What is more, there is nothing to prevent the judicial vicar leading the legal department as a whole, and often that would seem to me to be desirable. This is because he has built up considerable expertise in an inner-church environment.

THE CHURCH TRIBUNAL *PRAETER LEGEM:* FURTHER CONSEQUENCES

The ideas set out above demonstrate that setting up a legal department does not always have to be a utopian dream. The traditional tribunal operates in a wider context, but at the same time preserves its own specific character. The costs involved are not an immediate deterrent, because most of them can be shared between a number of dioceses. Introducing the construction presented here is not, of course, entirely without its difficulties. Indeed there is no obligation whatsoever for church leaders to get involved with anything like a legal department. It can be guaranteed that those who do not believe in it will leave the existing situation exactly as it is. There is a strong likelihood that it will be chosen to maintain the *status quo* in the area of tribunals. Why? Bishops usually have a preference for the pastoral side, and do not believe so strongly in structures. Nevertheless there are differences in approach here from one country to another. The Netherlands and Germany have much more of a structural approach than France and Belgium, for example[27]. In the United States, considerable attention has been devoted to special procedures for some time[28]. Nevertheless, immediate pastoral concerns often take precedence. Another reason that hinders innovations in the legal domain is precisely a thoroughgoing and often implicit choice in favour of canon law as a *ius perfectum* in which, see canon 1752, the salvation of souls must be the supreme law. And is the salvation of souls promoted by well-built legal structures? It is often said that these only promote individualistic aberrations.

At least that would be the plea of a devil's advocate. The fact that law and pastoral care do not contradict each other but actually confirm one another, is a position that does not require further argument here[29].

---

[27] Nevertheless, exciting ideas about a canon law which is not too developed structurally have been expressed, particularly in the Netherlands. See P. HUIZING en B.A. WILLEMS, "Sacramentele grondslag van kerkrecht", *Tijdschrift voor Theologie* 1976, 244-262.

[28] On the successes and problems, see V. VONDENBERGER, "Effective Due Process Is Possible in the Church", *Studia Canonica* 1996, 163-176.

[29] See the speech by Pope John Paul II to to the Roman Rota, particularly numbers 2, 4 and 7, *AAS* 1990, 872-877. For comments on this, see T. RINCÓN-PEREZ, "Juridicidad y pastoralidad del Derecho Canónico. Reflexiones a la luz del discurso del Papa a la Rota Romana de 1990", *Ius Canonicum* 1991, 231-252; J. LLOBELL, "I principi del processo canonico: aporia, mimetismo civilistico o esigenza ecclesiale?", *Il Diritto Ecclesiastico* 1996, 125-143.

Debates on this subject are, in fact, often sterile and abstract[30]. So here is another question: what would be the consequences of setting up a legal department? What is involved here is not so much setting out again the aims leading to its establishment. On the contrary, it is useful to analyse briefly a number of rather indirect consequences. I can identify at least four.

1. The development of a "multicultural" canon law.

The legal department applies a system of *open boundaries* in the field of law. That which is foreign, *in casu* secular law, is no longer mistrusted. It is no longer associated with expensive legal bills, when the fortress of canon law is threatened from the outside. In the new construction secular law is already in the picture, albeit modestly, from the time when specific legal texts are drawn up, namely at the rather unspectacular level of prevention. In this way law becomes *multicultural*. By multicultural I am not referring to differences of colour and taste characterising local canon law, based on the customs of different peoples or varying traditions within a particular church. The term *multicultural* refers to the integration of two completely different ways of dealing with law, namely the secular method and the *ius perfectum* of canon law[31]. The central question here is: how can canon law retain its own character while still coexisting peacefully with the secular legal system, which acts as a backdrop[32]? The multicultural society in legal terms.

2. Calling-card for people on the fringes of the church and outside.

The legal department does more than just avoid or undermine conflicts within the church. It is also a calling-card for the outside world. If the department is well structured and the legislator defines its role sharply against that of the secular courts, making it clear that there is no intention to create a parallel circuit in the wake of the *privilegium fori*, it can smarten up the church's image. People on the fringes of the church

---

[30] In particular the contradiction between pastoral care and criminal law is often strongly emphasised. See on this subject V. DE PAOLIS, "L'applicazione della pena canonica", *Monitor Ecclesiasticus* 1989, 70-73.

[31] J. LLOBELL, *l.c.*, 143.

[32] Cf. the conclusions of K. LÜDICKE, *l.c.*, 69-70.

or outside will probably be pleasantly surprised to find a high-quality, transparent legal department[33].

These days many people no longer have even a minimum of knowledge and education in the area of religion. In the social scene, however, law is ever-present, now as an icon of individualism, and now as an emancipatory force. Everyone gets involved with the law at some point. So a religion that can come up with a credible approach to law increases the credibility of its activities and even, indirectly but unmistakeably, of the content of its ideas.

3. An indirect influence on thinking within the church.

The external impulses that come from a legal department can also have an influence on the climate of thought within the church. The danger of standing still that exists within a closed system is no longer really such a threat when outside influences can filter in, for example through a legal department. Unrest and confusion are negative concepts in the church. They also have a positive counterpart, however, and they are then called movement and a wealth of ideas. At a time when the church is tending in many European countries to decline in numbers and to seek the safety of its own niche, the legal department offers a window on the outside world. Looking through it can reveal how rest sometimes points to a lack of life, and unrest to a high level of vitality. Law can then colour the life of the church in a way that goes far beyond the limited legal framework[34].

4. The changing profile of the canon lawyer.

The setting up of something like a legal department has an influence on the profile of the canon lawyer. As long as most practicing canonists work exclusively in the area of marriage law, canon law remains a *ius*

---

[33] The first category is, in theory, involved in the formation of public opinion in the church. The second is not. On public opinion in the church, see H. SCHWENDENWEIN, "Der Einfluss der öffentlichen Meinungsbildung auf rechtsgestaltende Massnahmen", *De Processibus Matrimonialibus* 1999, 117-144.

[34] That influence is often positive, but it can also be negative. See Bishop F. KAMPHAUS, "Was Gott verbunden hat...", quoted by N. RUF, *l.c.*, 401: "Mehr als früher ist heute zu prüfen, ob eine Ehe gültig zustande gekommen ist... Der Rechtsweg ist wichtig, das Allheilmittel ist es nicht. Er darf von den Betroffenen nicht mißbraucht werden, in dem die Realität dem Recht angepaßt wird."

perfectum whether it likes it or not. The combination of the principle of the indissolubility of marriage on the one hand and the emergency exits that nevertheless exist in canon law, often leads to an image of the specialist in marriage and marriage procedural law as a tight-rope walker[35]. He rides the track between theology and law, between the specific character of canon law and general legal technique. Here is an example: invalid legal acts are commonly found in secular law, but marriages which are null and void are relatively rare in that field[36]. People no doubt find a church tribunal which invalidate marriages fascinating, but certainly in Europe it remains a way of dealing with law which is seen as highly atypical.

It should be understood: jurisdiction on marriage no doubt has its place within canon law. It must stay. In the proposals set out above it will certainly not lose its significance, only its exclusivity. The other activities that take place within the framework of the legal department, however, have one point in common: they require closer contact with secular law. This immediately also means that a new canon lawyer needs his training to include general basic legal training and also a thorough introduction to Church-State relations, considered from the perspective of secular law. A course on the latter subject should create clarity on the room for manoeuvre and autonomy enjoyed by churches within the confines of a system of secular law. This definition of the problem is a logical consequence of the abandonment of the idea of the *societas perfecta*, combined with the intellectual courage to resist the temptation of an all-embracing *ius perfectum*.

Of course the canonist remains a canonist first of all. He does not need to be a gifted exegete and a sharp secular lawyer as well. Being a genius is only one of the options. The canonist must keep in mind the famous series of questions – which also give the title to an excellent painting by Paul Gauguin: *D'où venons-nous? Qui sommes-nous? Où allons-nous?* For the first question a good basic theological insight is

---

[35] Some people are calling for a clearer attitude in this connection. See, for example, F. DANEELS, "Überlegungen zum kirchlichen Ehenichtigkeitsprozess", *De Processibus Matrimonialibus* 2000, 29: "Weil andererseits der Ausdruck "nichtige Ehe" keineswegs bedeutet, daß nichts gewesen sei, wird nicht geleugnet, daß im Fall einer ungültigen Ehe irgend ein anderes Band als das Eheband bestehen könne. Ich meine jedenfalls, daß wir zweideutige Formulierungen bei der Vorstellung der Ehenichtigkeitsverfahren vermeiden und klar zum Ausdruck bringen müssen, daß sich diese Eheverfahren auf das Bestehen oder Nichtbestehen des Ehebandes von Anfang an beziehen."

[36] On the nullity of legal actions, see the classic work by O. ROBLEDA, *La nulidad del Acto Jurídico*, Rome, Libreria Editrice dell'Università Gregoriana, 1964, viii + 358 p.

needed. Most church leaders are in agreement about the need for this. *Qui sommes-nous?* refers to the canonist's understanding of himself. The principle here is that a canon lawyer must always question his own position and what he does. That means always, and not only in periods of crisis, although during the past forty or fifty years that amounts to the same thing. The third question, *où allons-nous?* (also, but not exclusively) has to do with the role of secular law in putting canon law into practice. The canonist must know, or know how he can find out, what the nature and consequences of his actions are in terms of secular law.

A modern canonist must, from his training onwards, pick up the thread of secular legal thinking once again. Those canon lawyers who look with suspicion at any real link with the world of secular law or consider this to be completely undesirable, prove, paradoxically enough, that they have missed the boat in the theological domain. That is because an enemy of secular law conceals, behind his apparent pastoral compassion, a deep nostalgia for the *societas perfecta*.

FINAL THOUGHTS

The story above is about church tribunals. It can be read on two levels.

On the first level it becomes clear that the universal law does not allow the facet of *jurisdiction* to develop adequately as a third section and final piece in the *trias politica*. One remedy is to draw a vertical line alongside the horizontal line between the three powers. How? Through the setting up of the legal department, which comprises, alongside the traditional church tribunal, also the special procedures and the prevention group. The legal department provides structural added value, for a more credible church, for a point of contact with secular society.

On a second level, the formation of the legal department also comprises a *statement*. A *statement* can be a reason for not bringing about something which is essentially positive. What is involved here? A positive option for a church which is no longer a *societas perfecta* and therefore welcomes certain of the *acquis* of secular law without any complex. It should also resist the temptation to replace the *societas perfecta* by a *ius perfectum*, to withdraw to a sub-cultural island with a law of its own. In this sense the setting up of a legal department also implies theological choices. The abandonment of the *societas perfecta* idea during Vatican II is made concrete in canon law at the level of the particular church. At the same time, the legal department contains a message towards the future: the dialogue with the secular world is not a passing fashion dating from the 60s of the last century. Canon law is keeping the borders open and opting for a multi-cultural legal culture. That is exciting, it makes people slightly uneasy and it creates a little confusion, but on its deepest level it is essentially Catholic.

PERSONALIA

JAMES A. CORIDEN was born in Hammond, Indiana, USA in 1932. He earned an S.T.L. and a J.C.D. at the Gregorian University and a J.D. at the Catholic University of America. He has taught canon law for more than thirty years and has published several articles on canonical issues. He wrote *An Introduction to Canon Law* (1990), *The Parish in Catholic Tradition* (1996) and *Canon Law as Ministry. Freedom and Good Order for the Church* (2000) and served as one of the editors and authors of *The Code of Canon Law: A Text and Commentary* (1985) and of the *New Commentary on the Code of Canon Law* (2000). He is professor of church law and dean emeritus at the Washington Theological Union.

ROCH PAGÉ was born in Chicoutimi, Québec, Canada in 1939. He studied canon law in Rome (JCL, Gregorian University, 1967) and Ottawa (JCD, Saint Paul University, 1968 and PhD, University of Ottawa, 1969). Following his studies, he served in the diocese of Chicoutimi as spiritual director at the seminary, as a defender of the bond at the diocesan tribunal and judge at the regional tribunal of Québec until 1977, at which time he began teaching as an assistant professor in the Faculty of Canon Law at Saint Paul University. In 1983, he was named full professor, and since 1993 has taught as a guest lecturer for a month each year at the Catholic University of America in Washington, DC. In 1996 he was named Dean of the Faculty of Canon Law at Saint Paul University. R. Pagé has published books, contributions to commentaries on the Code of Canon Law, and numerous articles.

RIK TORFS was born in Turnhout, Belgium in 1956. He studied law at Louvain University (lic. iur., 1979; lic. not., 1980) and Canon Law at Strasbourg and Louvain University (J.C.D., 1987). After one year of teaching at Utrecht University (The Netherlands), he became professor at the Faculty of Canon Law (K.U. Leuven) in 1988. Dean of the Faculty of Canon Law since 1994 and visiting professor at the University of Stellenbosch (South Africa) since 2000, R. Torfs published seven books and more than 200 articles on canon law, law, church and state relationships. He is editor of the *European Journal for Church and State Research*.

PUBLICATIES / PUBLICATIONS
MSGR. W. ONCLIN CHAIR

Editor RIK TORFS

Canon Law and Marriage. Monsignor W. Onclin Chair 1995, **Leuven, Peeters, 1995, 36 p.**

R. TORFS, *The Faculty of Canon Law of K.U. Leuven in 1995*, 5-9.
C. BURKE, *Renewal, Personalism and Law*, 11-21.
R.G.W. HUYSMANS, *Enforcement and Deregulation in Canon Law*, 23-36.

A Swing of the Pendulum. Canon Law in Modern Society. Monsignor W. Onclin Chair 1996, **Leuven, Peeters, 1996, 64 p.**

R. TORFS, *Une messe est possible. Over de nabijheid van Kerk en geloof*, 7-11.
R. TORFS, *'Une messe est possible'. A Challenge for Canon Law*, 13-17.
J.M. SERRANO RUIZ, *Acerca del carácter personal del matrimonio: digresiones y retornos*, 19-31.
J.M. SERRANO RUIZ, *The Personal Character of Marriage. A Swing of the Pendulum*, 33-45.
F.G. MORRISEY, *Catholic Identity of Healthcare Institutions in a Time of Change*, 47-64.

In Diversitate Unitas. Monsignor W. Onclin Chair 1997, **Leuven, Peeters, 1997, 72 p.**

R. TORFS, *Pro Pontifice et Rege*, 7-13.
R. TORFS, *Pro Pontifice et Rege*, 15-22.
H. PREE, *The Divine and the Human of the Ius Divinum*, 23-41.
J.H. PROVOST, *Temporary Replacements or New Forms of Ministry: Lay Persons with Pastoral Care of Parishes*, 43-70.

Bridging Past and Future. Monsignor W. Onclin Revisited. Monsignor W. Onclin Chair 1998, **Leuven, Peeters, 1998, 87 p.**

P. CARD. LAGHI, *Message*, 7-9.
R. TORFS, *Kerkelijk recht in de branding. Terug naar monseigneur W. Onclin*, 11-20.

R. Torfs, *Canon Law in the Balance. Monsignor W. Onclin Revisited*, 21-31.
L. Örsy, *In the Service of the Holy Spirit: the Ecclesial Vocation of the Canon Lawyers*, 33-53.
P. Coertzen, *Protection of Rights in the Church. A Reformed Perspective*, 55-87.

Church and State. Changing Paradigms. Monsignor W. Onclin Chair 1999, Leuven, Peeters, 1999, 72 p.

R. Torfs, *Crisis in het kerkelijk recht*, 7-17.
R. Torfs, *Crisis in Canon Law*, 19-29.
C. Migliore, *Ways and Means of the International Activity of the Holy See*, 31-42.
J.E. Wood, Jr., *The Role of Religion in the Advancement of Religious Human Rights*, 43-69.

Canon Law and Realism. Monsignor W. Onclin Chair 2000, Leuven, Peeters, 2000, 92 p.

R. Torfs, *De advocaat in de kerk, of de avonturen van een vreemdeling in het paradijs*, 7-28.
R. Torfs, *The Advocate in the Church. Source of Conflict or Conflict Solver*, 29-49.
J.P. Beal, *At the Crossroads of Two Laws. Some Reflections on the Influence of Secular Law on the Church's Response to Clergy Sexual Abuse in the United States*, 51-74.
Ch.K. Papastathis, *Unity Among the Orthodox Churches. From the Theological Approach to the Historical Realities*, 75-88.